Meridian Hill

Meridian Hill

A HISTORY

STEPHEN R. McKEVITT

Charleston · London

THE
History
PRESS

Published by The History Press
Charleston, SC 29403
www.historypress.net

Copyright © 2014 by Stephen R. McKevitt
All rights reserved

First published 2014

Manufactured in the United States

ISBN 978.1.62619.572.1

Library of Congress CIP data applied for.

Contents

Acknowledgments

Working on this history has been something of a voyage through time for me, and through the city as well; it has been an enjoyable trip. There are a number of people who have helped me with this endeavor, at times pointing me toward some of the city's resources, at times correcting me when necessary, and offering their opinions and advice. These welcome interactions have been part of this interesting voyage, and so, thank you to all. First, I am grateful to historian Kenneth Bowling, who has been most generous in sharing his superb understanding of the history of early Washington, D.C.'s many facets. A thank-you to Washington historian Matthew Gilmore, coordinator of many history projects in the city, for his useful comments. At the Washingtoniana Collection of the Martin Luther King Library of the District, the personnel there were very helpful. The staff members of the Historical Society of Washington, D.C., have not only been of assistance, but have also given me encouragement—so thanks to Anne McDonough and a special thanks to Laura Barry, who has been especially helpful. A thank-you goes to Washington historian, mapmaker and computer whiz Brian Kraft, with his valuable compilation of the city's building records, and his knowledge of how D.C. has been assembled. Thanks to the staff of the National Archives, especially to Robert Ellis. And gratitude to the Library of Congress staff, particularly the people of the Geography and Map Room. A thank-you to the staff of the U.S. Commission of Fine Arts, where many pieces of the cultural history of Washington's past are now held. And a special thanks to Kim Williams, of the District of Columbia Historic

Preservation Office, who—with her wonderful knowledge of Meridian Hill's past—is a continuing advocate of today's Meridian Hill neighborhood.

And at The History Press, a thank-you to J. Banks Smither, who has given me needed helpful guidance as I have traveled along the interesting production path that has led to the publication of this book. Also at The History Press, thank you to managing editor Julie Foster, for effectively running the detailed preparation of this manuscript on to its finished composition.

But certainly, the content and the opinions that are contained within this narrative are of my own doing, and I am solely responsible for them. And thus, any errors or missteps found inside are also solely my responsibility.

Introduction

M eridian Hill is a neighborhood located in the northwest quadrant of Washington, D.C., just beyond the original area of the city that was laid out by the L'Enfant plan. It sits directly north of the White House. The expanse of land that makes up Meridian Hill—a bit over 110 acres—is situated between Florida Avenue and Columbia Road, and is approximately four blocks wide, running to the west from Fifteenth Street over to just before Eighteenth Street. Meridian Hill is a place, a home, an estate, a farm, a subdivision, a neighborhood, and a park. The following account is an exploration that looks at the story of this interesting locale from the earliest of times to the present.

This chronicle contains information from a range of sources about the people and events that have helped to shape the pieces of history that have formed the fabric of Meridian Hill. The narrative is intended to be inclusive, cohesive and accurate, as well as informative and, it is hoped, engaging.

Throughout its history, Meridian Hill—much due to its prime location in the city—has been an appealing spot where many have chosen to reside. Today, with the worldwide need for energy conservation, which urban living can help provide, and with the practical convenience that also comes with city living, Meridian Hill continues to be an attractive part of Washington. This account here, however, concentrates primarily on the basic but interesting history of the neighborhood itself and how it came to be put together and, to a lesser extent, on the diverse stories of the many individuals who later chose to reside in the area; there is much more to be explored at Meridian Hill.

In the present-day world of Washington, the full footprint of the old Meridian Hill estate is something that is not always readily apparent. Major changes over the years have altered much of its area, with newer names on occasion being added on top of the old ones. Today, for instance, when some local D.C. residents go looking into their neighborhood's past, they might end up wondering just why Meridian Hill is being mentioned in the old records of the land along busy Columbia Road. The following story of Meridian Hill delves into the details of just what has occurred and why.

The narrative is generally chronological up until the time of the modern era, at which point the separate aspects of the area's story are each individually looked at in more detail. Throughout this account—but especially later on, when moving into modern times—not only are significant historical events covered, but also discussed are some of the evolving civic issues. Meridian Hill, a fairly small neighborhood, shares many of the same characteristics seen when looking at any similar community. Just about every neighborhood contains some intriguing bits of history—some occurrences that merit note, especially for the residents and those interested in that particular area. This history contains a generous number of these slices of information, but also some additional details that are there to function—in spots—at placing the locale and its happenings in a context that tracks its life in parallel with the growth of Washington. Because of its unique location and how it developed, Meridian Hill can reasonably be seen—if this is not too much of a cliché—to be something of a microcosm of the larger region that surrounds it.

STEPHEN MCKEVITT
Washington, D.C.

1

Early Times

A good point at which to start reviewing this location and its history is at the time in the past when the region's climate most recently became temperate, making the area a suitable place to live. The geography has been through many changes over the eons, being either land or water, and either hot or cold. But the modern world's landscape was basically established after the conclusion of the last major ice age.

This most recent worldwide glaciation had generally receded by about eleven thousand years ago. Meridian Hill's land then evolved into part of a forested territory; the site sits on the side of an incline that rises to the ridge of one of the higher terraces of the Potomac River, above a lower terrace whose border is outlined by the present-day curve of Florida Avenue. For some time after the ending of this icy era, the Potomac—with a larger volume of water—flowed through a series of these terraces, retreating gradually from the upper ones, until it finally reached its present-day flow and course. At its most intense, the last glacial period had an ice mass that came to within about 150 miles of the Washington area, down to around the middle of the present state of Pennsylvania. The cold climate that had then existed in the Potomac region can be characterized as a *taiga*, a harsh environment akin to the conditions that are now present in Alaska.

After the world's temperatures had progressively shifted upward, and the North American continent had then sufficiently warmed—and with the resulting temperate climate that covered the local area—the plants and animals that are now considered to be native moved in. These flourished abundantly on the favorable ground they found there, even well after the arrival of the first humans.

Archaeological evidence supports the thinking that the first modern humans came to live in this region perhaps seven thousand years ago. Prehistoric artifacts indicate that humans from Asia were on the North American continent more than thirteen thousand years ago, even before the ice had fully receded north, but it appears that the first local settlements occurred much later on. Those people then evidently dwelled in this area in a basic natural balance until the early 1600s, when several European groups ventured over and established their colonies along the coast of the Atlantic. About four hundred years ago, the tribes of the Native Americans living on the eastern side of the Potomac were generally known as the Piscataway, with a small local tribe being the Nacotchtank.

***

The land beneath the Meridian Hill area was originally part of the considerable expanse known as the province of Maryland, which in 1632 was granted by Charles I of England to Cecil Calvert, second Lord Baltimore. In this region of the new colony, the Potomac River at first essentially determined the location of settlements, and thus the first land grants that were allocated to the English settlers. Charles County, when established in 1658, was the early regional government and was much larger in size than it is today; it initially included the area that would become Washington, D.C., until 1696, when it was divided into two counties with the site of the future capital becoming part of the new Prince George's County.

James Langworth is considered to be the earliest owner of the land in the immediate area, with a grant dating from the original settlements for a tract of more than six hundred acres that included the locale containing the land of today's Meridian Hill. At his death in 1662, James willed this land grant to his son, John, who in 1664 recorded the grant's location; the tract was later patented, or registered, in 1686 by John's brother, William Langworth. William registered the grant in Charles County while he was living elsewhere in the county. It does not appear that the Langworths ever exercised their right to occupy the land of this grant—neither attempting to use it nor to build on it.

After William Langworth died in 1693, the land passed to his family, and in 1714, William's two daughters (Elizabeth and Mary) sold the patented property—which had been given the name Widow's Mite—to Thomas

Fletchall. Before long, Thomas's son, also Thomas Fletchall, split the land and passed on part of the grant, selling 206 acres of it to James Holmead in 1722 (for the price of thirty-eight pounds). In the history of the region, the involvement of these early individuals—before Holmead and the 1720s, when the actual settlement of the land started to occur—was mainly just a matter of official record of landownership.

James Holmead had his land patented in 1723; he would go on to become the principal landowner in this vicinity. Holmead's property, counting other land that he later added, amounted to many hundreds of acres on the east side of Rock Creek, going south from Piney Branch Creek and included much of the locales of Adams Morgan, Columbia Heights and Mount Pleasant. James entered into a number of land deals with other early settlers, including John Flint, his fellow vestryman at Rock Creek Church, which served as the area's first community social center. Following the death of James in about 1754, his lands were inherited by his nephew Anthony Holmead. Later, after Washington, D.C., was established in 1791, and then as the District grew, the Holmeads gradually sold off pieces of their property to new residents. Today, the family name lives on in several locations in the city, notably with the street entitled Holmead Place in Columbia Heights.

And so, when James Holmead obtained—and then actively took up—the ownership of a portion of the same area as the older Langworth grant, the modern history of the area effectively began. In what was essentially frontier territory, using a tract of land was often an important consideration when one wished to be deemed the possessor of that land. The Holmeads used the land, although sometimes a bit casually, and by additionally either giving or selling pieces of it to acquaintances and other settlers, they helped to create the beginnings of the neighborhood. (For more on James Holmead, see page 124.)

To the south of the Holmead property, Thomas Fletchall sold sixty-two acres in 1725 to John Bradford, who in turn sold this land to John Flint in 1730. Flint, a settler recorded as a yeoman (a mid-level farmer), would name the tract Flint's Discovery; this land, including a large 1735 addition to it (sold by a Henry Watson), was enrolled and patented by Governor Charles Calvert. Flint's property, which included the future site of Meridian Hill in its northern section, was a fair-sized piece of land, with its boundary on the south being down near present-day S Street in the Dupont Circle area. After being acquired, this tract was most likely farmed by John Flint and his family.

The first European settlers in the area, largely English, were a mix of a few large landowners, yeomen and indentured servants, plus a number of captured slaves. At times, a wealthy landowner, in order to receive grants of land, was obliged to pay the ocean-crossing costs for a group of indentured servants, who were then required to work the land of that property holder for a number of years, typically seven. After serving their time, these indentured individuals were then usually able to secure their own lands, but sometimes because of debts accrued, they were compelled to stay working on the landowner's property. The slaves generally did not have any other opportunities. The families of these various people often came as well; they endured dangerous sea voyages with notoriously high mortality rates. After the forested land was cleared, homes were built and food crops were planted. Then tobacco for export—with a newly established market in Europe—quickly became an important cash crop in the region.

Rock Creek

Because the area that would become Washington, D.C., was situated just below the first waterfall that was encountered by exploration ships coming up the Potomac, the location was selected as a naturally good spot on the river at which to stop and start a settlement. By 1703, a small outpost had been established on the riverside just to the west of the mouth of Rock Creek. The surrounding area—the land that lay north of the small inlet that would become the Tiber Creek—was then known for a time simply as Rock Creek. With the formal founding of Georgetown in 1751, just below the local geological fall line, the land on the hills and ridge that lay to the northeast of the town became a bit more easily accessible. An early nearby path allowed people to move along the ridge; today, this path is known as Columbia Road. John Flint's property lay just to the south of this nascent road.

Since it was on the ridge, this early route that eventually became Columbia Road very likely originated as a Native American trail; it offered a naturally good passage across the area because the ridge was a watershed divide, with no streams crossing it. The trail followed along the crest that separates the upper Rock Creek watershed from the lower set of streams flowing to the Potomac. After the European settlements were established and grew during the 1700s, the path of this trail developed as part of a route—initially known as Rock Creek Road—that ran between Georgetown and the cities to the north.

From the hillside and on the crown of Meridian Hill, the view to the south looking down to the Potomac River and beyond is superb. Undoubtedly, the Native Americans of the region, and later the new settlers, must have enjoyed the remarkable vista.

And what of the Native Americans? For a brief time after the actual onset of European colonization, the native people who had considered this area to be their home formed occasional loose alliances with some of the Maryland settlers, to at times oppose the more aggressive Susquehannock tribes who lived to the north. But by the end of the 1600s, just about all of the indigenous people were gone from this area, although a small number of them had been assimilated into the settler life in the slowly developing territory. The others had moved on to the west, or had been killed by the several new diseases introduced by the Europeans. Early documents report that the few natives who stayed separated from their tribes, and occupied menial positions in the settlements. It appears that this development of using a group of people—these native people—to work in servile jobs, and treating them as second-class humans without rights, set the stage for that which followed in America: large-scale slavery. This situation thus allowed a number of the European settlers in America to claim that it would be acceptable to plan and then create a culture that embraced finding more slaves—while crafting devious and deluded ways of ethically condoning the terrible and odious concept of slavery.

Records tell that these Native Americans, when first encountered, were engaged in agriculture, as well as hunting, with small permanent villages; the land near the river was fertile for their crops, and the area abounded with game. The local Nacotchtank tribe had a settlement (noted in the earliest colonial logs) on the Potomac about where Georgetown is now situated, with the other few native villages arrayed along the banks of the nearby Anacostia River. The Nacotchtanks, living alongside the larger tribal group named the Piscataway, are considered to have been a branch of the Algonquian peoples. Early records also report that area native families were often in turmoil as their social fabric came apart, with their leaders anxiously trying to work out agreements that would allow them to continue on with their former way of life.

A little to the north of Meridian Hill's land, on the banks of Piney Branch, a number of old stone arrowheads have been found alongside the rock formations there, showing that the area was being worked. As the region grew, these same rocky outcroppings were at times used to provide stone for some later colonial construction. In addition, when construction of Meridian Hill Park first began on the area's land, a number of early native artifacts were found and saved. City archaeologists today also believe that there are likely other older native relics buried along the former creek bed of old Slash Run, the creek that drained the nearby hillsides; this creek flowed all the way down to what is now L Street in the central city before eventually draining into Rock Creek. Present-day Kalorama Road from Sixteenth Street follows the route of Slash Run along where it went down toward today's Florida Avenue.

ROBERT PETER

In 1760, the land containing Meridian Hill's location changed hands again. Robert Peter, a leading area merchant who would later become Georgetown's first mayor, acquired the Flint's Discovery tract of land from John Flint's son, also named John; this was the tract, a few hundred acres in size, that lay south of the larger Holmead property on the south side of present-day Columbia Road. The Flints had possessed this land for little more than one generation; as was sometimes the case then, the property passed on to a merchant who was likely supplying the financial credit and the materials needed by the family to live on the land. (And separately, Robert Peter was also acquiring other tracts of land to the south of Flint's Discovery.)

Into the later 1700s, this general area remained a rural backwater; the famous and daring American ideas of self-government were mainly being developed elsewhere—largely within the major cities such as Philadelphia and Boston. But the national protests that were occurring just before the War of Independence were being discussed and broadly supported locally. The war would affect everyone, of course, but especially the wealthy, who had something to lose—or to gain—in any action. Most often, the merchants were Tory; that is, supporting Britain and the status quo. So after the Boston Tea Party action, a general regional meeting was held locally in June 1774, at Hungerford's Tavern (near today's Rockville, Maryland), with Georgetown's businessmen also invited to attend. At this meeting, a resolution was fervently agreed upon that stated the importation of English tea would not be allowed to occur locally until further notice. Two months later, the brigantine *Jane and Mary* from England arrived at the lower Potomac—with tea aboard that had previously been ordered by Robert Peter, wealthy merchant. Another meeting was then called, with the citizenry inviting Mr. Peter to attend; there at the gathering, with perhaps just a bit of social pressure (tactfully noted in the meeting record, where he is thanked a tad too profusely), he agreed to refuse to accept the shipment.

After the war's conclusion, and after much discussion, this locale was selected as the place for the new Federal capital—with Robert Peter being a strong promoter of the site, involved in the acquisition of its needed land. When architect and planner Peter L'Enfant laid out the city of Washington, present-day Florida Avenue—initially called Boundary Street—was designated as the city's northern limit; its route had been, and continued to be, part of the older Georgetown–Bladensburg Road. The land up on the hill north beyond this boundary was thus not included in the development plan for the city; still, this terrain became part of the new District of Columbia, in what was then called the County of Washington, so named to distinguish the outer sections of the territory from the specific platted-out city. The difficult task of surveying the District for the first time—and of also positioning the stone boundary markers—was undertaken by Andrew Ellicott in 1791 and 1792. [Architect L'Enfant, after coming to America from France in 1777, changed his name from Pierre to Peter and was then known as Peter, formally and informally, for the remainder of his life.]

Robert Peter, an adept and prosperous tobacco merchant who was then one of the wealthiest members of the community, had built a house on his Flint's Discovery tract of land not long after he had acquired it in 1760; described as a "log mansion house," the home was located a bit south of where Boundary Street was being sketched out by L'Enfant, and just east of today's Fourteenth Street. This broad tract that Peter then owned was christened Mount Pleasant, with the expanse of its prominent hill being identified as Peter's Hill (later to become Meridian Hill). At that time, the name Mount Pleasant referred to Peter's land south of Rock Creek Road; today's neighborhood of Mount Pleasant is situated a short distance north of this old thoroughfare. When this area to the north was first being settled, it was a somewhat later development and likely took its name from the nearby, older Peter property. After all, Mount Pleasant is a nicely agreeable descriptive title for a neighborhood.

Born in Scotland in 1726, Robert Peter had come to Maryland in about 1746 as an agent for the tobacco-merchant firm of John Glassford; he later went into business on his own, moving into many areas of local commerce. By some accounts, he was rather hardnosed. And as one of the major landowners in the region, Peter (simply moving beyond his Tory-related past) became an active and enthusiastic participant in the creation of the District of Columbia. From city records, it seems clear that he was quite satisfied and proud of his ownership of land in the new Federal City. He had several children, with Thomas, his eldest, later becoming involved in the early activities of the city. Robert Peter passed away in 1806. He may be best remembered today for his real estate holdings, but in one respect—with his meticulous attention to detail and record-keeping—he might have materially helped the new city move into the world of modern development.

The Peter and Holmead families were neighbors, and had very likely become related through marriage within their extended families, but it appears that there was some dispute between the families over title to a portion of the land north of Boundary Street, above the upper section of the new city. So in 1791, Anthony Holmead had his property surveyed; Robert Peter had his surveyed in 1792. (The two families apparently had a couple of other exact-boundary title disputes regarding land in the region. The old Flint property and the Holmead lands appear to have been unclearly intertwined; resurveys went on for several years.) The agreement that they reached in this location resolved that Robert Peter held ownership to the area south of Rock Creek Road—his large Mount Pleasant tract—and that the Holmead lands (then named Pleasant Plains) lay to the north of this road. This resolution covered the lower section of county land, up to where Rock Creek Road turned to the northeast. Thus, at the time of the founding of Washington, D.C., Robert Peter's property included the land that would become Meridian Hill.

**

The District of Columbia, by Andrew Ellicott, 1794. A key map, this well-crafted work gave the country its first detailed look at the entire designated area of its new capital. *Library of Congress.*

By the early 1800s, and running up on the crest of the hill above the city, the old Rock Creek Road—rustic ancestor of Columbia Road—had become named Rock Creek Church Road because it led to and past the old Rock Creek Church, which was situated farther up the thoroughfare at the location of today's historic Rock Creek Cemetery. The church parish had earlier been founded in 1712, when the region that would become Washington was first being socially organized. In 1719, land fronting on the road had been given to the parish for the building of a church, and for the subsequent creation of the cemetery.

After 1805, the portion of this road that went by the future site of Meridian Hill was next being called Old Tayloe's Lane (almost immediately "corrected" to be written Old Taylor's Lane). This stretch of the road had been named for John Tayloe, who, in 1802, had provided funding for the construction of a large and popular racetrack that was situated just to the north of the present-day intersection of Fourteenth Street and Columbia Road, sitting on land leased from the Holmeads. Tayloe, a wealthy Virginian and builder of the historic Octagon House, also had a two-hundred-plus-acre estate named Petworth, farther up the road to the north and east (not far from the church), in what is now, unsurprisingly, the neighborhood named Petworth. And in the Petworth area today, the still-in-use winding stretch of the same-named Rock Creek Church Road is, in fact, a remaining piece of this old route.

2

The Origins of Meridian Hill

As a distinct location with its own distinct name, Meridian Hill came into existence in 1816, when the land became the estate of David Porter. His decision to name the tract Meridian Hill was directly tied to its geographical position, sitting due north of the recently built White House.

COMMODORE PORTER

After the end of the War of 1812, Commodore David Porter, who had been active in the early naval operations of the new United States, decided in 1815 to relocate to the federal city of Washington, where he continued working for the U.S. Navy. Born in Boston in February 1780, Porter had grown up in a family that lived in the world of the sea. His grandfather, Alexander Porter, had commanded a Boston merchant ship prior to the Revolutionary War. David's father, also named David, was an active and noted captain in the Revolutionary War, commanding Continental navy vessels commissioned by General Washington.

In 1808, David Porter married Evalina Anderson of Philadelphia, and then, while living in Pennsylvania, they had started what would become a large family. Evalina, born in 1790, was the daughter of William and Elizabeth Anderson of Chester, Pennsylvania; her father would later be elected to the U.S. House of Representatives from Pennsylvania, after which he then served in a number of government positions. In addition to their own children, David and Evalina also adopted eight-year-old James (later changed to David) G. Farragut. Farragut would later go on to develop his own illustrious naval career.

David Porter entered U.S. Navy service early in life, as a midshipman in 1798, and was soon busy working in the center of the young nation's international seagoing activities. He participated in the Barbary Wars of 1801–07, serving briefly as a captain of the USS *Enterprise*. Later, while commanding the USS *Essex*, he was one of the key naval officers responsible for successfully harassing the British navy in the War of 1812, spending time in the Pacific striking at English whaling ships. And locally, after the burning of Washington in 1814, Porter famously rushed in to help drive the British out of the area around the devastated city. Following the end of the war in 1815, Porter was appointed to the three-member Board of Navy Commissioners, which had been newly established to manage the U.S. Navy. The year 1815 was an important time for Washington, D.C., with the city being rebuilt and the government developing its plans for the future.

In 1816, after finding and then purchasing a tract of 110 acres of land from out of the mostly empty expanse just north of the official city, Porter and his wife spent the next several years building a large home there, which they named Meridian Hill. This noted residence was designed to sit exactly north of the White House, and was placed on the rise just above Boundary Street. The land that became the Meridian Hill estate had earlier been platted out, and then sold in 1811 by Thomas Peter, Robert's son, to Washington Bowie (another well-to-do Georgetown merchant). Bowie in turn sold the tract to the Porters on March 20, 1816.

David Porter reportedly paid $13,000 for the property, a huge sum for that time. The money for this purchase came mainly from the spoils taken from vessels captured during the War of 1812. In the war, Porter, along with other naval commanders such as Stephen Decatur and John Rodgers, had amassed large amounts of "prizes" taken not only from the British navy's ships, but also from the independent privateers and merchant ships that they had encountered, fought with and captured.

In the nation during the early 1800s, there were proposals being advanced to declare the White House's longitude to be the prime meridian of the United States. So in 1804, on this due-north hill that Porter had purchased, Thomas Jefferson had had a marker placed to indicate the White House meridian. With civic pride, many citizens wanted America to generally set its own geographic and scientific standards in order to develop a clear national identity. When the new city was being planned,

David Porter (1780–1843). Oil portrait, possibly by John Trumbull. *Naval Historical Center.*

the president's house had been positioned very close to the center of the diamond shape of the District of Columbia; its site on a nearby ridge was chosen to best work with the topography and to provide a good view for the president. The District's diamond shape also presented an elegant geographical element for mapmaking. But after trying out an American prime meridian in the real world, the idea was fairly quickly abandoned because of confusion among other ships on the high seas. Then, too, the District's unique shape was later broken up when its western portion was returned, or retroceded, back to Virginia in 1846. Still, although never becoming the location for a U.S. prime meridian, the White House today remains a key focal point in the city.

Porter's new residence was situated right in the middle of what is today Sixteenth Street, just a bit south of present-day Crescent Place, and about one and a half miles north of the White House. The mansion was set on a dramatic knoll (known as an escarpment), quite a bit higher than the level of today's roadway. (When Sixteenth Street's path up the hill was later created, the prominence was cut lower so that the grade change could be evened out.) The large house, built of brick and stone, faced south with a broad front portico that had four dramatic stone columns; its design has been attributed to George Hadfield, noted early federal city architect who also created Washington's first city hall.

After Meridian Hill was completed in about 1819, David and his wife, Evalina, soon became famous for their social and political entertaining, a bit of which is described later on in a couple of excerpts from a book written by their son, David Dixon, who was later himself an important officer in the U.S. Navy (becoming the second American sailor to attain the rank of admiral, after his adoptive brother, David G. Farragut). During this time, the Porters spent lavishly, living within the fairly small world of Washington politics and society. The country was then becoming more confident about the course of its future after the conclusion of a war that did not undo the democracy that had recently been created, and the citizenry could certainly be in a more positive mood. With a mansion and money, Evalina moved into the social whirl of the fairly new city, and unfortunately—with David away for long periods—she became the subject of rumors of infidelity, which, true or not, apparently put a strain on their marriage.

Using the estate's land adjoining his new home, Commodore Porter also became a gentleman farmer while still engaged in his naval activities. The property was quite large for its location so close to the city; officially, the estate was recorded as being 110¼ acres (44.62 hectares) in size. It was situated as follows: starting on its east side, about 50 yards (46 meters) east of where Fifteenth Street now runs, it extended over to the west for a bit less than four-tenths of a mile (about 640 meters) to a creek where Champlain Street is now located. From Boundary Street, it went up to its northern border along the present-day Columbia Road, a distance of almost half a mile (about 780 meters).

Some interesting slices of information about Meridian Hill can be found in the 1875 book *Memoir of Commodore David Porter, of the United States Navy* by David Dixon Porter, the commodore's son. Two excerpts from the book follow. The first is from page 265:

> Considerable prize money had fallen to the lot of Rodgers, Decatur and Porter, and they determined to build residences in the District of Columbia. Capt. Porter accordingly purchased a farm of 157 acres on the heights, about one mile due north of the president's house, which being directly on the meridian of Washington, he called Meridian Hill. Here he erected a large and elegant mansion overlooking the city of Washington and the broad Potomac. The chain of hills, on which the house was built, forms an amphitheatre around the city, and were, at the time, covered with a fine growth of forest, the whole forming an extensive landscape which, to this day, has lost little of its beauty. Here was to be found everything that money could procure, to make the time pass pleasantly after the life of toil and warfare through which Captain Porter had passed; and here he delighted to dispense that hospitality, which made his house a place of reunion for some of the wisest and greatest in the land.
>
> Decatur built an equally fine establishment on the corner of H Street and Lafayette Square, which is still standing; and here these distinguished officers, daily extending their influence with congress and the executive, were enabled to prevent the service from being affected by any lack of congressional information, and kept it up to high water mark by the arguments they could supply to the secretary in making his annual report. They were always mindful of the adage that "the way to a man's heart is through his stomach," and although their entertainments materially affected their financial resources, yet they were the means of bringing the naval officers in contact with the men who held the public purse strings, and who were not always inclined to be liberal where the navy was concerned.
>
> [In the War of 1812, both Stephen Decatur and David Porter had amassed sizeable amounts of spoils, which would become their personal wealth; at the time, this behavior was considered to be an acceptable conversion of war capture and likely also a not widely known fact.]

Porter's estate was officially recorded as being 110 acres in size, not the 157 acres mentioned above. See the note about this on page 122 in Chapter 11.

A second excerpt, from page 269, reads:

During his residence at Meridian Hill, Captain Porter became much interested in farming. His friend, Mr. John Skinner, was the editor of an agricultural paper, and the various hints in regard to the proper cultivation of the soil, the Captain endeavored to put in practice on his gravelly land, where crops did not seem to thrive. In truth, though an excellent sailor, he was no judge of land for farming purposes, though if he had suspected the existence of that deposit of white sand under his estate, which since the establishment of the board of public works has been made manifest, he might have made the place pay good dividends. James K. Paulding, an intimate friend of Captain Porter, in his amusing book, John Bull in America, good naturedly satirizes the nautical hero's system of farming.

All sailors imagine themselves competent to manage a farm, and are never satisfied until they own one. The historic Pennsylvania Dutchman may not have understood the theory of farming, but in practice he was certainly successful, for what vegetables he could not sell, he gave to the pigs, and what the pigs wouldn't eat he ate himself. The Captain on the other hand, was so proud of his farming, that he supplied his acquaintances with the best of vegetables for nothing. He had a kitchen garden of five acres, and had to buy vegetables for winter; he had a hundred acres in corn, oats, wheat, &c., and was obliged to purchase grain for his stock. He imported English bulls, at twelve hundred dollars apiece, people would not patronize them. He had the finest piggery in the country, but alas, it did not pay. Thousands of cart loads of manure were hauled upon the farm, only to be washed away by the spring rains; the place was in beautiful order, highly satisfactory to the casual observer, but it yielded absolutely nothing.

The Captain then introduced an English farmer on the premises, established him with his family in a beautiful little farm house, and supplied him with half a dozen assistants. At the end of the year, the crops realized just about enough to pay the expenses of this party, without any overplus in the way of profit. On the whole, Captain Porter found that he had been more successful in ploughing the sea than he was ever likely to be in ploughing terra firma. Still his farming was a great source of recreation to him, and not wishing to let it run down he formed, in company with a few friends, a joint stock company for the purpose of running a horse boat between Washington and Alexandria. This scheme promised to be a great success, as the only communication between

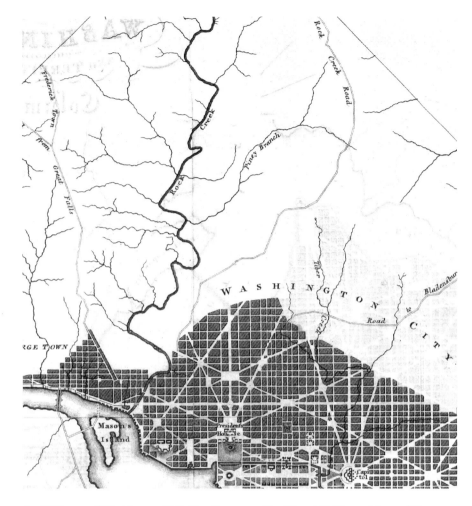

An 1819 map of Washington, D.C. (detail), engraved by W. and D. Lizars. *Library of Congress.*

the two cities was by a lumbering old stage coach, but the speculation ultimately proved a bad one. The new mode of conveyance was slower than the old coach, and the boat frequently gave out on the journey; the Captain gave free tickets to all his friends, and after awhile the ferry boat was withdrawn from the route and used for transporting passengers from Georgetown across the river, to Analostan island.

There is also mention that silkworms might have been raised on the farm—a mostly unsuccessful enterprise fad of that period. It certainly seems likely that Porter would have been interested in something novel such as this, a truly modern American application. And in fact, in the neighborhood today there are still some older mulberry trees, which are specially grown as a habitat for silkworms.

***

David Porter had several difficult years following 1822, with the Porters eventually losing Meridian Hill through foreclosure after their marriage had fractured, and after, David had returned to the sea, involved primarily with fighting pirate activity in the Caribbean. Three factors seem to have prompted his decision to leave Washington in 1823. First, although very capable, he did not enjoy a job that basically involved captaining a desk and daily having to deal with the political maneuverings endemic to the nation's capital. Second, America's commerce was being harmed by illegal operations off its southern coast. And third, the Porters, after having spent lavishly, were running out of money; David likely expected that some captured plunder might help remedy this problem.

So, after resigning his position as a navy commissioner, Porter took command of a small force (dubbed the Mosquito Fleet) and went to Caribbean waters to combat the pirates. There, amid its many islands, he had some real success in numerous adventures, enduring much adversity. His actions against these buccaneers greatly aided the U.S. economy, but he also created some personal enemies; thus, upon his return to Washington in 1825, Porter was quite unfairly court-martialed in a highly contentious trial, accused of over-aggressive action in dealing with well-entrenched lawlessness in the West Indies, and for later insubordination. At an island town that was basically being run by a pirate faction, Porter had gone ashore to forcibly retrieve one of his men who was being improperly held in jail. The island, of course, was Spanish territory, and this action was taken without any diplomatic communication or approval. This exploit could well have resulted in a minor scolding for Porter, but he had had some prior personality conflicts with a few other U.S. Naval officers—and these were the officers who ended up overseeing the trial. Porter's frank opinions also apparently did not help with the outcome. Additionally, Spain was unhappy with the developing situation in the Caribbean. Spain well understood that it had a only a tenuous hold on some of the islands there and knew that Porter's successes at sea had driven some of the pirates out of the water and onto land, where they continued with their illegal activities—on Spanish land.

The court-martial was a major event in Washington, and the subject of quite a number of comments, both political and personal; it caused many members of Congress to take sides. Both Andrew Jackson and John Quincy Adams put forward their opinions, with Jackson supporting Porter, and Adams opposing him. This situation polarized the trial. In the end, after receiving a six-month suspension from duty, Porter chose to resign from the navy.

In 1826, and in dire economic straits, Porter accepted an offer of employment from Mexico and left the United States to lead the Mexican navy, a move that almost ended in disaster. While there, and with the chaotic conditions then present in much of Mexico, he clashed with some of the leaders (including General Santa Anna), who were, at times, ruling through the use of corruption and intimidation. Porter was very nearly killed in an assassination attempt. When he returned to the United States in 1829, the widespread feeling in Washington was that he had been treated unjustly at his court-martial, where his diplomatic infraction had been inflated and used for political purposes. So in 1830, just as he was losing his estate to foreclosure, Porter was offered a U.S. consulate position, which he took. He was then later offered the ambassadorship to the Turkish Empire, which he accepted and held until his death in 1843. History shows that Commodore Porter was a man of integrity and courage and was a true American hero. In addition, his life and deeds have provided the material for many of the stories that are told in the seafaring lore of the early history of the United States.

Evalina, who with her social connections and education undoubtedly had a large hand in the creation of Meridian Hill, lived on to be eighty years old, passing away in 1871. Sadly, she was apparently chronically in need of money; her son, renowned Civil War U.S. Navy admiral David Dixon Porter, assisted in finally getting her a government pension.

The memorial monument to David Porter at his grave site in the Woodlands Cemetery of Philadelphia reads, somewhat effusively:

> Commodore David Porter, one of the most heroic sons of Pennsylvania, having long represented his Country with fidelity as Minister Resident at Constantinople, died at the city in the patriotic discharge of his duty, March 3rd, 1843. His early youth was conspicuous for skill and gallantry in the Naval Service to the United States when the American arms were exercised with romantic chivalry before the battlements of Tripoli. He was on all occasions among the bravest of the brave, zealous in the performance of every duty, ardent and resolute. In the trying hour of calamity composed and steady in the blaze of victory. In the War of 1812

his merits were exhibited not merely as an intrepid Commander, but in exploring new fields of success and glory.

A career of brilliant good fortune was crowned by an engagement against superior force and fearful advantages which history records as an event among the most remarkable in Naval Warfare.

While his naval career was one full of gallant and successful deeds, his personal life was certainly hardly one of good fortune. But in the end, although David Porter spent only a few years of his life at Meridian Hill—perhaps less than six—he established the name and the locale, both of which still brightly live on to the present day.

***

A separate event occurred in early 1829, while the Porter family was in financial distress. Their mansion was leased for a brief time to John Quincy Adams, who had just lost the presidential election of 1828 to Andrew Jackson. Upon moving there, Adams had offered to purchase Meridian Hill from the family but was unable to do so; the Porters, having borrowed against the property, likely had mortgage entanglements. Adams apparently had unsuccessfully offered $14,000 for the property; he then resided there for only a few months. This rental agreement was somewhat unusual because, at that time, Adams and Porter were on opposite sides politically (Porter had supported Jackson), but with David then out of the country and with his wife Evalina estranged from him, and since also socially friendly with the Adams family, the rental occurred.

As it happened, John Quincy Adams was familiar with the neighborhood, since he had earlier invested in the local business known as Columbia Mills, which was situated on Rock Creek to the north of what is now Calvert Street. In 1823, shortly before he became president, Adams had assumed ownership of the mill when its then owner, his wife's cousin George Johnson, defaulted on the loans that had been provided by Adams (much to the president's chagrin, since the enterprise consistently lost money). This gristmill quickly became known as the Adams Mill, and was in use until about 1867, when it was dropped from the tax rolls; the mill's site, with nothing now remaining except a marker, is presently on the land of the National Zoo. Today, Adams Mill Road—its route very much repositioned—bears his name.

Justice Cox

Just before Meridian Hill's foreclosure in 1830, arrangements were made to sell the estate to J. Florentius Cox of New York. Cox came from a well-known family that had been among the early settlers of the island of Bermuda, where they had become a leading family. But before the time of the Revolutionary War, some members of the Cox family had relocated to mainland America. Trained as a lawyer in New York, and fairly prominent in society there, J. Florentius Cox may have moved to Washington with the intention of finding work with the federal government. In 1809, he married Eliza Lansdale, daughter of Thomas and Cornelia Lansdale, wealthy landowners of eastern Prince George's County. Major Thomas Lansdale had fought in several significant battles of the Revolutionary War and was at the Valley Forge military camp with Washington; later, after being held captive for a time, he ended his service in the war as a celebrated hero.

Along with the Cox couple, Eliza's brother Phillip Lansdale was also a co-purchaser of Meridian Hill and lived there until his death in 1840 at age forty-nine. Phillip had suffered a crippling spinal injury as an infant, with the result that he was also of a diminutive stature. It is likely that he had used his share of his family's money to help purchase Meridian Hill. With the somewhat prominent position that Meridian Hill held adjacent to the city, Phillip was also likely to have been known to visitors as being an integral part of the estate, lending a certain distinct and memorable quality to the mansion; thus, this could have been one of the various sources that over time have provided the literary fodder for dramatic stories and films about antebellum life in early America.

At the time of the sale, the estate was apparently in need of attention and maintenance, since it had recently been rented out and previously was being run with a limited budget. After the sale, contemporary accounts report that Cox was "making vast improvements." And J. Florentius Cox did indeed find employment in the District. By the mid-1830s, he had established himself as a well-regarded citizen of the territory, and by 1838, he had been appointed justice of the peace for the County of Washington in the District of Columbia; over the next fourteen years, he was reappointed several times.

Before it was incorporated into the City of Washington, the county was governed by a group of justices of the peace, who met in a levy court council. The justices performed the duties of county commissioners and, although not legally within Maryland, were subject to the Maryland state laws governing county commissioners. They not only administered local justice and decided civil cases, but also set local policies and taxes. The justices were appointed by the president, who also had the discretion to determine their number, typically between nine and eleven.

Justice Cox, with his wife and her brother, resided at Meridian Hill for a number of years, but in 1847, Eliza passed away. Cox remained there; however, in 1849, he put the estate up for sale, advertising it in the *National Intelligencer* newspaper as "Meridian Hill, an elegant mansion, with valuable farm of 110 acres." He did not sell the property at that time, though, and was still an active justice of the peace in 1851. Cox, who was born in 1784, continued living at the mansion for the rest of his life, and a later newspaper record tells that he died in 1858 "at his home, Meridian Hill." It was then disclosed that not too long before his death, Justice Cox had sold the estate to Colonel Gilbert L. Thompson, who became the next occupant of the property. But although he later took possession of the estate, Thompson did not remain its actual owner. As can sometimes happen with a piece of real estate, the ownership of Meridian Hill over the next couple of years developed into a slightly complicated situation.

In the years just before the Civil War, differing opinions in Washington were strong, and the city must have indeed been a place with an unusual ambiance. The city was a mixture of whites—who either supported or opposed slavery—free blacks, and slaves. Feelings, no doubt, could range from peaceful and blasé to uncomfortable, especially since the city had outlawed slave trading, yet the District was partially surrounded by a number of large slaveholding plantations. It was within this setting that Meridian Hill was being sold. The sale that resulted had the estate becoming less of a home and more of a piece of property. In 1856, Gilbert L. Thompson, along with William Dorsey from Baltimore (functioning as a quiet co-owner), purchased Meridian Hill; the two then sold the estate for $70,000 to Josiah Sturges in December 1856. Sturges in turn sold it in 1858 to Oliver Pettit of New York; thus, the property was being quietly owned by Pettit while it was thought of as Thompson's land. This ownership situation persisted so that in 1867, when another sale occurred, this somewhat hidden possession led to two lawsuits. (The events surrounding this sale are covered in the later chapter titled "The Modern Era.")

On an 1861 map of the District of Columbia by cartographer Albert Boschke, Thompson was recorded as occupying the land of Meridian Hill; the information contained in this fine map provides a snapshot of the District just before the Civil War. On the map, the estate's outline followed its original configuration, just north of Boundary Street, with the mansion

Map of Washington, D.C. (detail) by Albert Boschke, surveyed 1856–59 and published in 1861. *Library of Congress.*

being clearly noted. Thompson was shown on the map to be apparently continuing to farm a sizeable portion of Meridian Hill's land. (Although, in general—as many have discovered—the clay land in this area, after having been de-forested, continues to need fairly persistent attention to stay suitable for farming.)

Also shown on this map, and directly to the west on the other side of the property-line creek, was the neighboring farm of John Little, who had purchased that tract in 1836 from Christian and Matthew Hines. The Little family continued to own the property for many years, until modern area development started to occur. Earlier, in 1828, the Hines brothers had purchased this land abutting Meridian Hill from Anna Maria Thornton, widow of William Thornton, the first architect of the Capitol.

Gilbert Livingston Thompson, born in Washington in 1796, was the son of Smith Thompson, who had been secretary of the navy from 1818 to 1823, and was then later a Supreme Court justice. Gilbert was thus no doubt well familiar with Meridian Hill when he took possession of the estate. He also had other property (his primary home) in Maryland at Ellicott City near Baltimore, so he may have treated Meridian Hill more as a farm than as his residence. And newspaper accounts in the years just before the Civil War report that the mansion was then being used for social events and the mansion grounds for picnics.

COLUMBIAN COLLEGE

Separate growth was also occurring nearby. One instance of this growth was on the tract of land directly east of Meridian Hill, where, in 1821, Columbian College was established. It later became an important institution in the city. As a sign of its influence, consider this: By about 1870, the name for the old Taylor's Lane Road to the north (after a time of being called Georgetown Road) was being written finally with its modern designation of Columbia Road, likely in good part because the thoroughfare took people to the college. Columbian College sat to the south and west of today's intersection of Fourteenth Street and Columbia Road. The tract of 46.5 acres that became the college land had been purchased from George Peter in 1820 for $7,000; George was another of Robert's sons and had inherited the property after Robert passed away.

[The school was usually called Columbia College by city residents, and that name—also seen on the period maps shown on the pages here and upcoming—will be used for continuity in the remainder of this history.]

The college, which was located to the east of present-day Meridian Hill Park, had been chartered by Congress, and its creation fulfilled a proposed idea for a national university that had been made by George Washington, which he had first advanced when the District of Columbia was being organized. In his will, Washington left fifty shares of the *Potowmac Company* toward the endowment of such a school. Thus, in 1821, Columbia College's founding was considered—and rightly so—to be an important event for the young nation's capital. The college operated at this site until 1884, when it was moved to a new location in Foggy Bottom; in 1904, it was renamed the George Washington University.

A nineteenth-century engraving of the college's main building, which was completed in 1822. *Historical Society of Washington, D.C.*

As the new city of Washington had started to develop, one of the first early thoroughfares running due north outside the city was Fourteenth Street Road, an extension that went up to the racetrack at Taylor's Lane Road and then later, farther up and along to Peirce's Mill Road and to the farms beyond. Fourteenth Street Road had formed the eastern edge of Columbia College when the college first acquired its land. The school's property ran west from Fourteenth Street to a line just east of where Fifteenth Street is now laid out and, north from Florida Avenue up to Columbia Road, also including a very small tract directly across on the north side of the road. To the west of the school lay the Porter estate.

The proximity of the college to the Meridian Hill property is depicted in another snippet from the book *Memoir of Commodore David Porter, of the United States Navy*. From page 276, this story out of the past shows the timelessness of human nature:

> Next to the Commodore's place on Meridian Hill, the present Columbia College was established, which was in some respects a nuisance, the boys constantly trespassing upon the farm and robbing his orchard. Instead of complaining to the faculty, the Commodore one day went to the ground

where the boys were at play and called them around him. He told them
that he was sorry to see that some of their number were disposed to commit
depredations, that such things were dishonorable, and, that they might
have no excuse for such actions he would in future reserve for their use
the outer row of apple trees, about a quarter of a mile in length, warning
them not to trespass on the others. The youngsters gave him three cheers,
and promised to stick to the bargain. Only one of their number violated
the agreement, and he received a sound horsewhipping at the hands of the
Commodore. The culprit later in life became a member of congress, and
although he harbored no animosity against the Commodore, never forgot
the horsewhipping, and never afterwards liked the taste of apples.

During the early years of the school, Columbia College was often
in a definite bit of economic distress, with its endowment of shares in
the *Potowmac Company* having been lost even before that canal enterprise
faltered and was taken over by the C&O Canal Company. But several
years later, as the school flourished and expanded, it built or was given a
few other structures that were scattered throughout the downtown area of
the city. These included buildings for its medical school, which had been
established not long after the founding of the college. Its main campus,
however, remained situated next to Meridian Hill, there on the land that
the school had from the start called College Hill. Fortunately though, by
1850, the college was on a more sound fiscal and academic footing, in part
due to a number of bequests and some financial assistance from Congress.
Columbia College, a homegrown institution of learning, was continuing
to develop, becoming a genuine source of pride among the citizens of the
District of Columbia.

THE CIVIL WAR

With tensions nationwide rising even further after Abraham Lincoln was
successful in winning the presidential election of 1860, much of the country
was preparing for war. Just about all of the region surrounding Washington,
D.C., was affected when the war began in April 1861. And the Meridian Hill
estate would soon become involved in a major way.

By the beginning of the Civil War, the nation's political divisions had split
nearby Columbia College's faculty and student body, and the campus was in

Soldiers of the New York Seventh Regiment resting at Camp Cameron, 1861. *Library of Congress.*

quite a bit of turmoil. Much of its teaching staff and many of its students were from the Southern states and had left at the start of the conflict. In 1861, as the war effort enveloped the city, the college land on the hill—with its commanding position over the city—was quickly taken for use as an army encampment named Camp Cameron. As the camp was being set up, the military also took over part of what was by then the Thompson estate, including the large and well-appointed Meridian Hill mansion and a portion of its open land.

Many written accounts of life in the army during the Civil War have been published, stories telling of times in battle, and also of times spent with the day-to-day routines in camp. Some of these chronicles touch on the happenings at Meridian Hill, and clearly illustrate the difficulties of an extended war. The Civil War, though a necessary struggle, was a time of great tragedy for the country. One tale by a fresh recruit tells of his arrival at Camp Cameron when it was new, and relates how attractive the area

Service for Seventh Regiment of the New York State Militia at Camp Cameron, Washington, D.C., on Sunday, May 5, 1861. *From* Harper's Weekly, *May 25, 1861.*

was, with gardens, trees and a beautiful mansion, newly set up as a hospital. Later in the war, another writes of the ugliness of the mud and horribleness of disease, and of the mansion being destroyed by casual carelessness and out of basic necessity. Open fires were being lit in its rooms by convalescing soldiers trying to keep warm, with some of the soldiers idly carving their initials into the home's woodwork.

In addition nearby, many of the college's buildings were being badly damaged as the military activity expanded, and when the school later regained the property after the end of the conflict, it never fully resumed use of the campus.

With the war continuing, another military encampment, named Carver Barracks, was set up along Fourteenth Street Road on the northern portion of the Columbia College land. This collection of simple frame buildings and tents housed regiments that protected Washington during the war years, and also served as a staging area for troops passing through the city on the way to battle sites in the region. In correspondence of that time, this camp was almost always referred to as being situated at Meridian Hill, since the estate was then a prominent location marker in the District. Carver General Hospital was also established there, one of the many temporary hospitals set up in Washington to care for the war wounded.

City of Washington from Beyond the Navy Yard, by George Cooke, 1833. A view from the southeast. *White House Historical Association (White House Collection).*

***

Before the Civil War, Washington was the small city seen above; during and after the war, a dramatic change took place, with the capital become a much more developed city. The angle used to depict Washington in this painting, looking from the southeast, presents a view that is not too often seen; it not only shows the young city very nicely but also depicts the mostly empty hills to the north of the White House.

3

The Modern Era

This section covers the conditions that arose—and the planning that was done—that allowed the Meridian Hill area to grow.

AFTER THE CIVIL WAR AND WITH A NEW OWNER

Following the end of the war in 1865, and with the civic planning and infrastructure construction work that was soon initiated by D.C. governor Alexander "Boss" Shepherd, Washington started to develop at a quicker pace. The dynamic industrial growth of the United States at this time caused a significant increase in the size of the federal government, and the District was expanding. Areas outside the original city were being formally surveyed and titled. District real estate records have documented the details of this new activity.

Washington plat map books have recorded how the land of the Meridian Hill estate had been defined and laid out as the Meridian Hill subdivision, a plan created in September 1867 for Colonel Isaac E. Messmore, who was the then-new owner of the property. This interesting real estate development, arranged by planners Hall and Elvans, consisted of the land of the original Porter estate, which had recently been occupied by Gilbert Thompson, and embraced all of its 110¼ acres.

Sadly, the old Porter mansion had been thoroughly ruined by a major fire that occurred in March 1866, just after the home's wartime use had ended;

the mansion was never renovated, and was eventually razed sometime in the early 1880s, not too long before the first steps were taken to properly extend Sixteenth Street to the north. It is truly unfortunate that Meridian Hill's namesake residence had existed as a home for only a little less than fifty years.

Colonel Isaac E. Messmore was a Wisconsin lawyer, and then a Civil War commander, who resided in Washington for only a few years beginning in 1865; he was notable for being an active civic booster, believing in the grand future that lay ahead for the United States.

Below is a piece of information about him from *History of Kent County, Michigan (Early Local Papers)* by Michael A. Leeson, discussing Grand Rapids, Michigan:

Isaac E. Messmore, sole proprietor and editor-in-chief of the Daily and Weekly Democrat, is 55 years of age, and claims to be an early settler of Michigan, his father being born in the city of Detroit, and residing in that city over 40 years. The years preceding his majority were a continual struggle for the wherewith to maintain life and obtain an education, one portion of the time working at the most laborious occupations to obtain means with which to support himself while pursuing studies, the other portion of the magnitude of such a struggle no one can judge but those who have undergone it; but success crowned his effort. Having decided to be a lawyer, he turned his attention to that profession, went through the usual studies, and graduated at the Richmond (Va) Law School. In 1850 he settled in Wisconsin, where he resided until 1862.

Originally, in politics, Col. M. was a Whig, and acted with that party as long as it maintained a distinctive organization; but upon its dissolution he abandoned politics, for a time. In 1861, he allied himself with the Republicans, and was elected to the Wisconsin Legislature that year. This year he was also appointed Circuit Judge of the 5th Judicial District of Wisconsin. At the breaking out of the Rebellion he went from the bench into the Fourteenth Wisconsin Regiment as Lieut. Col., and served in that capacity until the battle of Shiloh. He then resigned and returned to that State, when he was immediately appointed Colonel of the 31st Regiment of Wisconsin Volunteers. Becoming disabled on the field, he was sent to the New York City hospital, remaining six months, where he underwent a surgical operation.

He resumed his command just before the close of the war and went to Washington, where, upon the recommendation of General Grant, Postmaster-General Randall and Gen. John A. Rawlins (afterward

Secretary of War), he was appointed Assistant Commissioner of the Internal Revenue Department, discharging, in addition, the duties of Solicitor of Departments. He was, during that time, appointed by President Johnson one (and executive member) of the celebrated Metropolitan Board of the City of New York, which post he held 18 months, when the board expired by limitation, and he came to Grand Rapids.

In 1876, becoming dissatisfied with the course of the Republican party, he joined the Democracy, and took an active part in the Presidential campaign of that year, and also in 1880. In July, 1877, in connection with Gen. A.A. Stevens, he purchased the Democrat establishment, and continued the publication of the paper with his partner until May 26, 1881, when he purchased the interest of Gen. Stevens and became sole proprietor and editor-in-chief.

Perhaps none of the various proprietors or editors of the Democrat have been so widely known as Col. Messmore. Having resided in various States and taken an active interest in whatever tended to promote the progress of the locality in which he resided, he of necessity has become well known throughout the United States. As a writer he is sharp and incisive, and attacks what he considers wrong in any section or individual; and in the discharge of his duty he neither gives nor asks quarter. No paper in the State has had more prominence, or its opinions oftener quoted by friends and foes than the Democrat. His knowledge of every topic that has in the past agitated the public or is now before the people, and his masterly handling of the subject, give him a respectful hearing from every class of the reading public. He courts opposition, not for the sake of controversy, but that through argument the right may prevail. During his administration the Democrat has steadily advanced until as a news and political journal it is second to none in the State.

Isaac Messmore was born in August 1821 and passed away in Los Angeles in January 1902; throughout his life, he seems to have been something of a go-getter and approached key situations with enthusiasm and a deliberate and thoughtful, ethical sense of purpose.

During the Civil War, the regiment that Colonel Messmore commanded was active in areas to the south of Washington. After the end of the war, in 1865, his regiment participated in the Grand Army Presentation that took place in the District. The grounds of Columbia College (and some of the land of Meridian Hill, including the mansion) were still being used by the army as a camp, so it is reasonable to suppose that Colonel Messmore visited the area. He would then have become familiar with the Meridian Hill estate; after leaving military service in 1866 and being appointed assistant commissioner of internal revenue, he likely learned of the estate's troubled state of affairs.

At the war's end, Gilbert Thompson, the previous occupant, was clearly financially unable to return to Meridian Hill. In 1867, when the estate was sold, Thompson, who was then seventy-one (and who appears to have quietly sat out the war), was living at his original home at Ellicott City in Maryland, where he later passed away in 1874.

After Meridian Hill's heavy wartime use, owner Oliver Pettit simply wanted to be done with the property, and was willing to sell it for payment of money that would satisfy the estate's unpaid expenses and liens—about $15,000. Messmore contacted him in mid-1866, and they agreed to a sale of the property, which was completed on July 19, 1867. This transaction then resulted in two legal challenges, and it took the following several years for these legal actions to completely play out. Both of these lawsuits asked for money, both were found to be without merit and both were dismissed.

Records of the D.C. courts (now held at the National Archives) report on the details of these legal actions. The first suit, brought by Gilbert Thompson's son, Smith Thompson, claimed that Gilbert had purchased the estate with money belonging to Gilbert's wife, Arietta Tompkins (with the money coming from her wealthy family), and thus had no right to sell the estate. The suit rested on the matter of the earlier hidden sales initiated by Gilbert; this legal challenge was filed in 1872 and was dismissed in 1873. The second suit was filed by Josiah Sturges and his family and claimed that Sturges, when he sold Meridian Hill, was heavily in debt and thus had no right to sell the property. This case was filed in 1875 and decided in favor of Colonel Messmore in 1876, after Isaac had relocated back to Michigan.

With the old Porter mansion ruined by the 1866 fire, and its land damaged by the rough army use, the estate was very unsettled, so when Messmore purchased the property in its distressed condition, it was certainly likely that he saw an open opportunity to not only improve and help grow the city of Washington but also to perhaps make some money as part of the deal. (In December 1867, Messmore added Joseph Stevens as a part owner of the property, apparently to help with its expenses.) By 1873, Isaac had permanently moved away from the Washington area and, along with his wife, Margaret, resettled in Grand Rapids, Michigan.

The preceding biography of Colonel Isaac Messmore describes that he had developed friendships with some key people in the District, and he appears to have been a person who saw larger possibilities in situations. Thus, although in D.C. only briefly, he left his imprint on the city.

***

An interesting and well-made map of 1867 shows the Rock Creek Valley, and the region around Meridian Hill before the plan for its subdivision was set in motion. On the map, Messmore was recorded as the owner of

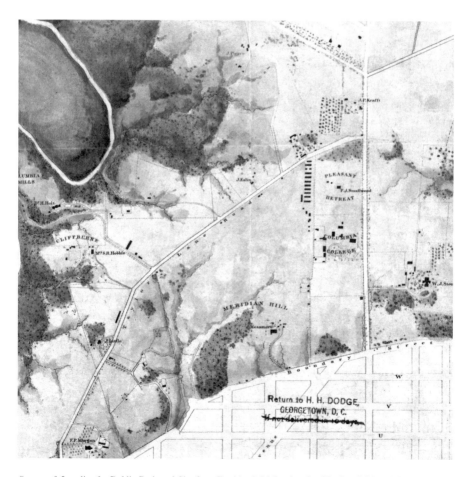

Survey of Locality for Public Park and Site for a Presidential Mansion, by Nathaniel Michler (detail), 1867. *Library of Congress.*

Meridian Hill, and the rural nature of the entire area can also be clearly seen. This work, *Survey of Locality for Public Park and Site for a Presidential Mansion*, was produced by Colonel Nathaniel Michler for the U.S. Senate as part of a grand proposal to relocate the residence for the president to the Rock Creek area of the District. While the idea never went beyond an initial consideration, it did lead to further thought regarding the merits of the creation of a large park in the beautiful Rock Creek Valley. After much discussion and much work by many people, Congress eventually followed up on Michler's report and established Rock Creek Park in 1890.

HALL AND ELVANS

After the Civil War, Isaac Messmore—who was new to the Washington area when he came into possession of Meridian Hill—apparently sought out people who could assist him with developing the land of the estate. Richard M. Hall and John R. Elvans were local businessmen in the city at the time and together were becoming involved in the new real estate ventures in the burgeoning Washington of the late 1860s, as the city was expanding beyond its original boundaries.

John R. Elvans, active in the municipal life of the city, was a successful hardware and building-supply store owner, public-spirited citizen and real estate investor who was a strong supporter of equal rights for former slaves. He assisted the Freedman's Bureau in purchasing Barry Farms, in southeast Washington, which the federal government then subdivided into farms for newly freed slaves. As a member of the city council, Elvans supported voting rights for blacks and cheered the first black voting in 1867. He also worked as a real estate broker with several of the other land developments that were then occurring outside the central city. Very much involved in the D.C. business world, Elvans was the secretary of a trade group that formed a city Mercantile Exchange in 1865. And in 1866, just north of downtown, at 928 M Street, he had a fine home built that was designed by noted progressive Washington architect Adolf Cluss.

Richard M. Hall, in a deposition from April 1870 in connection with the sale of property for Howard University, stated that his profession was a real estate agent. At the time, he had an office on Louisiana Avenue near the city's municipal center. Additionally, he also worked with John Elvans in developing other tracts of land, including the historically important Barry

Farms project. Records show that, as a team, the two were working with former Civil War army leaders on some of these new ventures. Their public statements also reveal that both shared the forward-looking civic ideals espoused by Governor Alexander Shepherd.

So together, Hall and Elvans were the individuals who did the basic organizational work that was necessary in creating the Meridian Hill subdivision, and then started the marketing of the separate lots in the development. Looking at the records from that time, it is reasonable to speculate that in this partnership, Elvans provided the business contacts, the financing and the cooperation of city hall, and Hall provided the legwork needed to begin the actual sales. The lots were then offered, apparently without great success, as being for sale "over time."

Following this spate of activity, the two men seem to fade from historical records. In the city, the 1874 removal of Alexander Shepherd as governor had a major negative impact on the progressive direction of city politics. Additionally, the nation at that time was experiencing a series of financial disruptions that might have adversely affected their lives, or the two might have relocated to a different region. After Governor Shepherd left office, largely because he had overspent on civic infrastructure improvements, thus sending the city into bankruptcy, he moved from the area to Mexico. There, he very successfully went into silver mining. It is total speculation, but it may have been that Hall and Elvans, who were friends with Shepherd, followed him south to Mexico.

In general, these early subdivisions were not the money-makers that the developers had usually expected them to be, so after some time with the project, Messmore, along with Hall and Elvans, appears to have turned the whole enterprise over to various real estate investors. Lots were being sold, but they were apparently being purchased by speculators and others who had little interest in developing their new property, thus inhibiting the subdivision's growth. By the 1890s, when development of the area had finally picked up, the empty lots west of Sixteenth Street were generally still owned by these assorted groupings of people, mostly local citizens and small real estate firms holding the lots as investments. And after 1895, of course, Mary Henderson would dramatically transform the eastern half of the subdivision's land with her remarkable buildings and grand plans.

ON THE LAND BEFORE
CITY-REGULATED CONSTRUCTION

Before the modern development of the subdivision began to occur, the area sat just partially used for a number of years. On the land's eastern side, during the Civil War and immediately after, the army facilities on the college property had attracted freed African Americans looking for protection and employment. In addition, the Thompson farm at Meridian Hill had previously held some slaves—not many, evidently, but some. By the war's end, a black community had been established on the east side of the farm, and not long thereafter, homes for them were being built along the new street, which was then named Columbia Avenue (it would later become Fifteenth Street). By the 1870s, a number—perhaps a few dozen—of small but adequate and secure frame houses had been erected on a small cluster of the lots there, along with a couple of stores. This construction was apparently sanctioned by Messmore, Hall and Elvans, the layout's planners—this being a way of advancing African Americans and the city itself into a sensible future. (These homes sat mainly on land that would later become the northeast area of Meridian Hill Park.) In addition, on Columbia Road at Sixteenth Street, a public school for black children was built by the city.

In 1875, Wayland Seminary—with a substantial four-story brick building—opened on Columbia Avenue to train African American Baptist clergy and teachers. This school was part of a larger effort to assist the freed slaves because great numbers of blacks had been generally left on their own, unassisted, and with no job skills, opportunities or education. The seminary remained there until 1897, when it moved to Richmond and merged with Richmond Theological Seminary to form the Virginia Union University. Mary Henderson also had her plans for future projects on a large portion of the eastern side of the subdivision. And then, after the government had formally decided in 1910 to acquire the pieces of land necessary for its planned park, the residents in this section were all displaced, with this occurring just after 1910. Some of them relocated nearby, to the western area of the subdivision—still segregated but also still within Meridian Hill—moving to homes in the area just north of Florida Avenue. And at this same time, three apartment buildings for African Americans were constructed along Seventeenth Street just north of Kalorama Road.

Some houses of African Americans in 1910, shortly before being torn down for the construction of Meridian Hill Park. *U.S. Commission of Fine Arts.*

Additionally, west of where Sixteenth Street would be laid, some scattered homes had also been built, probably at first in the early 1860s for workers involved in the city's war defenses, with many of the individual lots then having their own wells for water. Later, into the 1880s, this area became populated with both black and white residents in separate sections, and contained several dozen small frame houses. But these structures seem to have been generally constructed in an informal ad hoc manner; after 1880, when building permits had become necessary, the construction costs listed for some of them were a meager $300 to $500 each. And almost none of these structures appeared to have survived into the mid-twentieth century, though it is possible that a few of them—those already in place before the subdivision's creation—helped to define the positioning of the streets in the new layout. And so, while various parts of the tract were being used, a large portion of the land remained vacant.

Joaquin Miller and His Log Cabin, 1883

The 1883 appearance of Joaquin Miller and his log cabin just west of Sixteenth Street was a minor event in the area's history, but is something that is occasionally noted and is part of the larger Joaquin Miller story. Miller was a true colorful character of the nineteenth century—determined, clever, entertaining and, above all, charming. A writer, he made influential friends and traveled widely, mainly promoting himself as a rustic frontiersman of the West. After a stay in England, where he was fêted by the wealthy, he returned to the United States with his eye on obtaining the same treatment from Washington society. So in 1883, he had a rustic log cabin built on Crescent Place, where he resided for two years. After only limited success in D.C., he left this area, went west, and later settled in California. In 1912, when the essentially bogus cabin was going to be razed to make way for new construction, California's congressmen intervened and had the cabin saved and relocated to Rock Creek Park, where it remains to this day. The Park Service reluctantly agreed to accept this "gift," no doubt mindful of the source of its own funding. Joaquin Miller was possibly the best early prototype of today's media folks who are noted celebrities for being noted celebrities.

Miller, as one of the most famous American poets of the late nineteenth century, was renowned for his flowery, superficial and generally overwrought verse. Some scholars believe that his influence on poetry in the United States was truly toxic to the art form, so much so that it caused many Americans to

The Joaquin Miller cabin on Crescent Place in 1912. *Library of Congress.*

become completely averse to even the mere concept of poetry. Be that as it may, he is now regarded as a minor poet. His life was much more interesting, both here and on the West Coast. He eventually built a home, which he idiosyncratically called The Hights, outside of San Francisco, where he famously entertained his friends and fans for the remainder of his years. Born in 1837, he passed away in 1913.

THE GROWTH OF THE CITY

The development of the area of the subdivision occurred simultaneously with active growth in other parts of the city, which was moved forward by the technological improvements then being introduced. These included the installation of water and gas lines, an effective sewer system, and major street improvements, which were initiated in the 1870s by the very active Alexander Shepherd. In 1873, Shepherd was appointed the second governor of Washington, D.C., after the District government had been reorganized by Congress in 1871. Shepherd was born in Washington in 1835, and early on had gone into the plumbing trade, learning the business from the bottom up. He had quickly moved ahead, eventually first running the board of public works, and then the District itself. Shepherd was perhaps the most influential and productive single person to have worked on the basic infrastructure of modern Washington. Within the brief period of time from 1871 until 1874, with bold plans, he made extraordinary street and utility improvements to the city, unfortunately bankrupting the District in the process. This created major problems with Congress, and so in 1874, Shepherd was rather abruptly removed from his position as governor; after his firing, he later moved to Mexico and there successfully developed a complex and lucrative mining operation. He passed away in 1902.

To those interested in D.C.'s history: the story of Alexander Shepherd's life is worth exploring. Washingtonians who know about him know of the dynamic history of his short but important time here as governor, and they also know that he was nicknamed "Boss" Shepherd to signify his strong control of D.C. politics (and for the charges of corruption and cronyism leveled against him). It can at times be enlightening when coming across some little-known piece of the planning that he sponsored, which helped improve the city. Washington, D.C., is much indebted to him.

Even after Governor Shepherd's period of time in D.C., the District's growth continued, with new technologies being introduced. As the city's streetcar lines were quickly electrified beginning shortly after 1890, electric lighting power was brought into city neighborhoods. By the early 1900s, electricity had become available for home use in most parts of the Meridian Hill area. The 1890s generally were a time of great innovation, and the creative and practical applications of electric power (although at the time not always being used carefully) were developing into the very important part of the city infrastructure that modern society today takes for granted. Compared to New York City, Washington then did not have the same large accumulation of resources available for experimentation and installation, but still, with the District's position as the national seat of government, and with many powerful people proud of the work and the appearance of the U.S. government, much growth did occur. The newest ideas and the most up-to-date pieces of technical information were almost always passing through the city.

In addition, the freshly generated wealth that was then flowing into the economy of the United States—from the country's land resources, from newly organized businesses and from the results of an unprecedented technologically driven industrial revolution—had an almost explosive effect on the growth of parts of Washington. Some newly rich individuals, moving to D.C. as elected members of Congress or coming to be near the seat of government, had the opportunities to explore stylish construction possibilities with exuberant, elaborate homes. And obviously too, Mary Henderson, locally, was preparing her plans for the well-designed and beautiful structures that she later developed and built for eventual embassy use.

Other new residents, most of them with families, came as part of the emerging middle-class population, with their livelihoods often being in commerce or in professional work. These citizens created comfortable lives for themselves and their families with solid and secure homes in a community that they supported and enjoyed. And still others who moved into the area were members of the city's modern and stable working class, engaged in helping to build and maintain the municipality. There were still the larger unresolved social issues in the country, of course, but locally people and families were increasingly able to create a warm sense of place with a proud hometown feeling.

The Meridian Hill land was laid out, as was the nearby Lanier Heights subdivision, with some imagination and perhaps a bit amateurishly and before the city established planning rules in 1888, which were created in an effort to standardize land use and extend the original city grid concept to all areas of the District. (In 1871, the city of Washington had been officially expanded to include all of the District of Columbia, taking in Georgetown and the land of the county.)

The neighborhood's location up on the Columbia Road ridge was being touted in sales brochures as healthy and fresh, above the old lower city. By 1900, all of the well-made new residences in the District were being built with modern bathrooms, with electricity coming shortly. Locally, well-stocked and up-to-date grocery stores opened; marvelous fancy motion-picture theatres were being constructed; and easy and quick public transportation was available to take residents downtown to world-class department stores, such as Woodward & Lothrop, as well as to the city's other new shops. And for the newfangled automobiles, parking was being arranged, both on-street and in garages along planned alleys behind the homes. In 1890, as a sign of this growth, Boundary Street was renamed Florida Avenue.

With a new and impressive Beaux Arts city hall—christened the District Building and dedicated in July 1908—the city government crystallized and matured, displaying a strong civic stability; its departments became more uniform and vigorous. The police, the schools and the fire department became well organized and reliable. (The nearby firehouse just north on Lanier Place also opened in 1908.) Real estate record-keeping improved, and importantly, building codes evolved, with new rules for safe and sanitary housing. Building projects became regulated, with city-issued permits necessary for major construction beginning in 1877. With this civic pride, Washington—including its Meridian Hill area—was setting the stage for the positive, future United States development that occurred later in the twentieth century.

THE SUBDIVISION: NEW LAYOUT OF THE LAND

How did the neighborhood configuration that exists today come about? The following is an overview of the development of the Meridian Hill property as the Hall & Elvans Subdivision was initially planned in 1867. Not long after Isaac Messmore acquired the old estate, the tract was resurveyed by the city surveyor's office, with the resulting new plat map being recorded on September 18, 1867. This fresh official plat was then used as the base upon which the detailed plan for the subdivision was laid out. This subdivision layout, also created in September 1867, was drawn up and then printed as a large-format map. Later versions of this real estate map were used as posters in the sales effort to market the individual lots.

The Streets in the Subdivision

NAMES. On the original plat map, key streets were named for major U.S. lakes, mainly the Great Lakes. Some of these names are still in use today, but others were changed when the District regulated its naming system so that the horizontal streets would be alphabetical, with the same name across the region. Each of these names would also have an increasing number of syllables, as the alphabet was repeated moving away from the city center; in this area, these streets have two syllables. Thus, the original Erie Street, to the south of Columbia Road, was renamed Euclid Street in about 1906. And nearby Huron Street became Fuller Street. This naming scheme was implemented where practical, with the many obvious exceptions and alterations seen today. As a result, some of the streets in other nearby neighborhood subdivisions (Columbia Heights, Lanier Heights, Mount Pleasant) have also had two—and rarely, even three—different names since being laid out.

Why take the names of the Great Lakes? It seems reasonable to believe that Isaac Messmore, a native of Michigan and active in Wisconsin, would have been proud of these mighty bodies of water that were so important to the central region of the country.

NORTH/SOUTH STREETS. Down the middle of the area, logically, ran Central Avenue (now Seventeenth Street). One short street was named Messmore Avenue (now Mozart Place). On the east, Columbia Avenue went north from Fifteenth Street, and Meridian Avenue ran north from Sixteenth; by 1890, these names had been changed to Fifteenth and Sixteenth Streets to go with the city's system. At the western edge of the tract, following the old property-line creek, was Champlain Avenue (now Street), and next to Champlain Avenue lay Ontario Avenue (now Road).

ARRANGEMENT. A map of the area shows that some of the streets run at odd angles, ignoring the city grid. The basic reason for this is that the topography of the land offered natural and practical—but not straight—roadways at several locations. A few of these streets were in use even before the subdivision was drawn up. For instance, Kalorama Road—originally named Superior Street—follows the creek bed of old Slash Run, which went down the hillside toward Florida Avenue. Similarly, Ontario Road and Champlain Street both generally follow the contour of the land, being laid out in a slight gully that travels to the south. On the western side, the property line runs along the alley behind the west-side lots of Champlain Street.

The eastern property line was angled slightly to the northwest; thus, the street that later became Fifteenth Street was bent a bit onto a "collision course" with Sixteenth Street, and the intersection of these two does in fact occur several blocks north of Meridian Hill. At the east edge of the tract, this extension of Fifteenth Street also curved a little to the left to allow for additional building lots on the east side. Just west of the damaged Porter mansion, the paths of the short, curving roads likely predate this plan and were positioned as they are now due to the placement of earlier structures on the old estate. And finally, the other (new) streets were drawn up in blocks designed to accommodate the lot sizes chosen for the subdivision.

Some twenty-five years after its creation, this self-contained, somewhat unpolished layout came to be not that well-regarded by civic leaders— especially when the city's transportation planners were trying to create an orderly street arrangement for the entire District. After several years of discussion, Congress decreed in 1893 that D.C. should not only expand its original city grid to include all of its area but also realign (or more to the point, neaten) the nonconforming streets in the District's several older, free-form neighborhoods. But the city and its engineers, facing stiff opposition and legal challenges, succeeded in changing already-set road configurations at only a few D.C. locations. For the future however, the Permanent System of Highways Act of 1893 had a defining effect on the city.

The Real Estate in the Subdivision

The land's layout consisted of twetny-two blocks, called squares, with the standard size of each individual lot being 50 feet by 150 feet, although many lots were larger. The square numbers (keeping their original lot numbers) were later changed when they were incorporated into the District's master real estate system, which occurred when the defined street-grid plan was adopted city-wide. Thus, for example, Meridian Hill Square 14 became D.C. Real Estate Square 2565.

Early Growth of the Neighborhood

As the subdivision slowly evolved, the individual lots in it were generally purchased in groups, mostly by local people, and were built on from two main corridors. Sixteenth Street and Columbia Road were the major influences, as they now continue to be. The new construction that occurred formed distinct areas as the neighborhood developed, and created the basic makeup that exists today.

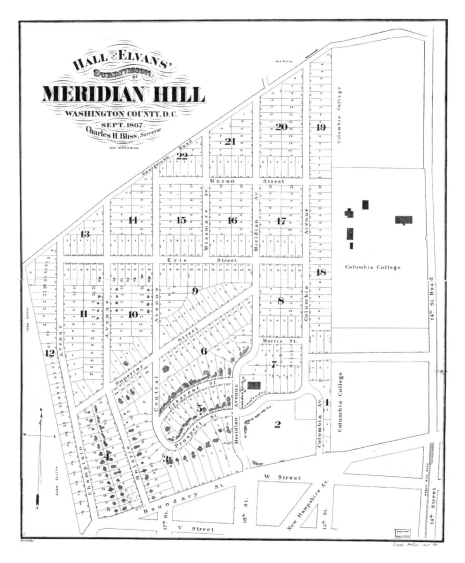

The subdivision of Meridian Hill, surveyed in September 1867. *Library of Congress.*

Hall and Elvans's subdivision plan for Meridian Hill laid out the new arrangement of roads and individual lots on the property. The subdivision was surveyed and drawn up by Charles H. Bliss in September 1867, done in preparation for the anticipated real estate sales of the lots.

4

Twentieth-Century Development

In the late nineteenth century, there had been only limited and sporadic growth occurring within the Meridian Hill subdivision, but by 1900, significant development had begun to take place, in part because the city in general was expanding. Some grand apartment houses would soon be erected in the area, and Mary Henderson was planning her projects along Sixteenth Street. The remarkable Henderson Castle had been built—its creation had commenced in 1888. A streetcar line established along Columbia Road in 1897 further encouraged expansion.

One interesting "might-have-been" idea regarding the neighborhood: In 1901, when the city of Washington was being significantly rearranged and improved with new civic works, the Senate Park Commission (with its McMillan Plan) seriously considered a proposal to create a large, completely circular park at Meridian Hill. It would have been centered on Sixteenth Street and would have encompassed, quite literally, the land from between Florida Avenue up to Euclid Street, a quarter of a mile in diameter. That certainly would have changed the neighborhood!

But other activity happened. By 1925, the neighborhood was essentially in place, and by 1950, it was mostly filled in.

***

What follows is an overview, by no means all inclusive, of Meridian Hill's modern-day growth, focusing primarily on the first half of the twentieth century. When examining the area, it seems reasonable to trace its development by looking first at those two corridors, which were its major stimulus points—Sixteenth Street and Columbia Road—and then take a look at the inside streets, where a quieter, more working-class growth occurred. (Henderson Castle and the building projects undertaken by Mary Henderson are covered in the separate chapter about Mary and her endeavors.)

SIXTEENTH STREET: GRAND AND EXCEPTIONAL

Before Sixteenth Street was extended beyond Florida Avenue, the curving road named Meridian Avenue (laid down in 1873) only generally continued the line of this key city street northward. Having Sixteenth Street developed—properly laid out and then skillfully constructed— was an important event in this area's history, and an influential step in carrying the city grid to the rest of the District. Planning for the street's extension was finalized in 1899, with the work commencing in 1900. The construction of the large, well-designed bridge spanning the Piney Branch Valley, north of the Mount Pleasant neighborhood, essentially established Sixteenth Street as a major artery. The span was finished in 1908.

After 1905, when the neighborhood's destiny was effectively set by Mary Henderson, some large and magnificent homes were built near the planned Meridian Hill Park. Mary sought to limit the number of apartment buildings in the area (and their height), but was less than totally successful. Thus, with her vigilant approval, some of them were constructed, such as the striking and opulent Meridian Mansions (now the Envoy) at 2400 Sixteenth Street, which was created by developer Edgar Kennedy and designed by architect A.H. Sonneman. It was D.C.'s largest and most costly apartment house when completed in 1917, with a price tag of almost $1 million. For the next several decades, Meridian Mansions—with its ballrooms and rooftop pavilions—was the setting for many social and diplomatic events.

On Crescent Place, just north of Henderson Castle, two extraordinary homes were built, both designed by noted architect John Russell Pope. The first, the White-Meyer House, at 1624 Crescent Place, has been home to two well-regarded Washington families. The property was purchased in 1910 by prominent American diplomat Henry White, who had been ambassador to Italy and France. The red brick Georgian home was completed in 1912, at a cost of more than $150,000. After White

Meridian House at 1630 Crescent Place. *Photo by the author.*

died in 1927, the property passed to his son, and in 1934 Eugene and Agnes Meyer, owners of the *Washington Post*, purchased the house. The second home there is Meridian House, at 1630 Crescent Place, built by Ambassador Irwin Boyle Laughlin, heir to a steel mill fortune. He purchased the land in 1912, two years after his friend Henry White had bought the adjacent site. After a long and notable career with the U.S. Foreign Service, Mr. Laughlin retired in 1919 and built Meridian House, filling it with his collections of art. Both homes are now occupied by Meridian International Center, a nonprofit organization promoting worldwide cultural understanding.

Flanking Meridian Hill Park on Fifteenth and Sixteenth Streets, and on Crescent Place, are several well-made deluxe apartment buildings, the more elaborate of which were erected not long after the park's lengthy construction period commenced in 1914. In later years, some simpler and more prosaic apartment houses were added as the population of D.C. increased. The generally fine architectural designs of these buildings add to the beauty and depth of the city and nicely demonstrate the different architectural styles that were prevailing at the various times the structures were built. Most were constructed from 1920 through the 1960s. One good example is the Embassy Towers (1931), a five-story Renaissance Revival–style building of brick with limestone trim at 1620 Fuller Street—a thoughtful, solid building that would be an asset to any city neighborhood.

At 1661 Crescent Place, there is a quiet but notably attractive six-story brick Georgian Revival apartment house, designed by architect Joseph Younger and developed by brothers Monroe and R. Bates Warren. It opened in 1926 as a cooperative. Built with three wings extending back from the street, it features large, well-detailed apartments. The site layout created rather generous grounds, with tranquil gardens, making it a desirable address. It attracted upper-level members of the State Department and the military. The Warren brothers, along with their two uncles, Bates and John Warren, were Washington-area developers and builders who created a number of fine apartment houses, both nearby, and then later in other D.C. neighborhoods. (Interestingly, the building permit for this address notes that its height was objected to by Mrs. John B. Henderson.)

The Dorchester House, an impressive and prominent apartment building at the top of Sixteenth Street's hill, was designed by architect Francis Koenig and built in 1941; it stands as a distinctive example of the Art Deco style. This noted and handsome 395-unit building is positioned overlooking the park, at 2480 Sixteenth Street, between Euclid Street and Kalorama Road, and sits on land that was originally owned by the Hendersons. After completion, it became a popular home for some members of Congress who needed a place in Washington. The property has recently undergone renovations, which should keep it an attractive address into the future.

Meridian Hill Hall on Sixteenth Street. This graceful building was constructed in 1942 as the Meridian Hill Hotel. *Photo by the author.*

At 2601 Sixteenth Street, sitting well positioned just north of the park, is Meridian Hill Hall, a fine apartment house also built in the stylish Art Deco motif, and created by architect Louis Justement. Erected in 1942 with government wartime assistance, it opened as the Meridian Hill Hotel for Women, offering many amenities such as air conditioning. It is now owned by Howard University and has become a residence hall for university students. Earlier and interestingly, as part of Mary Henderson's larger plan for the area, this site was intended to be the location of a new French embassy; a building design for this was created, but construction never occurred.

Next is the Warder-Totten Mansion at 2633 Sixteenth Street. In 1915, architect George Oakley Totten Jr. built a house for himself in the Arts and Crafts style at the rear of this address. Then, from 1923 to 1925, in an early preservation action, he moved and reconstructed the Benjamin Warder House, designed by H.H. Richardson in 1885, from 1515 K Street to the front portion of his lot, combining it with his own house. Totten rescued and used

The Warder-Totten Mansion at 2633 Sixteenth Street. *Photo by the author.*

The Italian embassy at 2700 Sixteenth Street, seen about 1925. *Library of Congress.*

the original exterior stone (except for the main doorway) and much of the interior woodwork of the Warder home. This sandstone mansion, originally built in a Romanesque Revival style, is one of the few remaining Richardson buildings in the city. In 1972, this address, with both houses, was listed on the National Register of Historic Places. After being neglected for years and almost ruined inside, the structure has recently been renovated and has now been converted to apartments.

At 2700 Sixteenth Street, on land purchased from Mary Henderson, sits the elaborate Renaissance-style building that was formerly the Italian embassy. Built in 1925, it was designed by Warren and Wetmore of New York, and built by James Stewart and Company. This four-story, thirty-five-thousand-square-foot building, which is a stately and superbly detailed work of architectural art, was designated a historic landmark in 2006; there is now work underway to repurpose the property into apartment homes, adding a stylish new addition on land in the rear at Seventeenth Street.

A bit north, at 2800 Sixteenth Street, is the Scottish Rite Temple, completed in 1939. This imposing and formal stripped-Classical limestone structure features a highly decorated front entrance. It was designed by architects Porter, Lockie & Chaletain and built by the Charles H. Tompkins Company. The building brings a serene and solid presence to its block.

The private mansion at 2829 Sixteenth Street was designed by architect Nathan C. Wyeth for Emily Eames MacVeagh, who built this beautiful structure (secretly, as a surprise gift!) for her husband, Franklin, and her family. Erected in 1910 by the George Fuller Company, it cost an extraordinarily pricey $120,000. In 1921, it was purchased by Mexico for use as its embassy, and is now home to the Mexican Cultural Institute.

Among the other apartment houses along Sixteenth Street are two nicely made specimens: the Diplomat (1940) at 2420 Sixteenth Street—an eight-story, 112-unit building, designed by architect Joseph Abel in the fairly basic International Style but with good attention to detail—and the stylishly attractive 125-unit Park Tower at 2440 Sixteenth Street, which was designed in 1928 by William Harris, and is now a condo building.

Also on land purchased from Mary Henderson is the Cuban embassy, at 2630 Sixteenth Street, a handsome three-story Neoclassical-style stone edifice designed by noted Washington architects MacNeil and MacNeil, and built in 1916 for the government of Cuba.

In 1977, a development named Beekman Place was constructed on the site where Henderson Castle had earlier stood. Although not especially distinguished architecturally, this calm and pleasant village of 216 condo

The MacVeagh Mansion at 2829 Sixteenth Street, not long after its completion in 1910. *Historical Society of Washington, D.C.*

The Cuban Embassy at 2630 Sixteenth Street, as it looked around 1937. *Library of Congress.*

town homes added stability to the neighborhood after they were built, bringing new residents to the area.

The Bustle of Columbia Road

Around this thoroughfare, and going east over into Columbia Heights, a solid and comfortable neighborhood was built, appealing to some of the professionals working in the city—as well as to government civil service individuals—the desk-job employees. Convenient streetcar service also increased the area's desirability. Because of the smart, close-in location along this higher point in the city, the homes of this area, both north and south of Columbia Road, turned out to be popular. They were typically well-made row houses with excellent details, and were constructed starting just after the beginning of the century, mostly between 1902 and 1912, and in fairly quick succession—speculatively, as demand warranted.

Near Euclid Street, a couple freestanding houses had also been built by 1905, and several apartment buildings, both low-rise and larger, were later constructed on the street and to the south. From number 1746 to 1756 Euclid Street there is a nice early stretch of row houses built in 1900 for Edward Childers, and designed by N.T. Haller. Next to these, at the corner with Ontario Road, is a solid six-story, sixty-unit apartment house (1740 Euclid Street) built in 1919, and designed by architect Claughton West. Anchoring the other corner of the block, at Champlain Street, is the Cortland, at 1760 Euclid Street, another six-story apartment building constructed in 1915 and designed by architects Hunter and Bell.

The prolific architectural firm of Hunter and Bell was active from about 1902 until 1918, just after the U.S. entry into World War I. These two architects created hundreds of residential buildings in the developing areas of the city. Little is known about the early training of Ernest C. Hunter and G. Neal Bell, but they both appear to have grown up in Washington. Bell did so in what is now Columbia Heights (likely having been born in North Carolina). In the center of the District, they left behind a fine legacy of handsome and solid buildings, designing row houses and apartment houses in a variety of styles, but mainly using the Classical Revival motif. Although their façades were traditional, they generally planned their structures using the most modern of construction techniques. Many of their larger buildings are of brick with a reinforced concrete interior, which was then a relatively new building method. After World War I, a related firm continued on for a brief time as Bell and Rich.

Along the south side of Columbia Road—the subdivision's upper edge—light retail structures, apartment houses, and churches were built. The churches are especially notable. Near Sixteenth Street and Columbia Road, on the southeast corner with Harvard Street, is the handsome, well-known All Souls Unitarian Church, designed by Coolidge and Shattuck and completed in 1924. On the southwest corner, at 2810 Sixteenth Street, is the elegant former Mormon Chapel, designed in 1933 by architects Young and Hansen; it is today a Unification Church. And down Columbia Road, at the northwest point of the old estate's land, is the impressive First Church of Christ, Scientist, located at 1770 Euclid Street and completed in 1912.

On the southeast corner with Ontario Road, at 1736 Columbia Road, sits Beverly Court, a four-story Classical Revival apartment house built by Bates Warren in 1915 and designed by Hunter and Bell; it is now a cooperative. At Seventeenth Street and Columbia Road, on a site that previously held a small Safeway, was the noted Ontario Theatre, built in 1951 by K-B Theatres. It opened as a popular and deluxe first-run movie house and later became a rock concert venue, finally closing as local tastes changed. In 2014, the site was redeveloped by the Peterson Companies and entitled Ontario 17, with a new and stylishly modern building of condo apartments and light retail.

East of Seventeenth Street, a few apartment houses were also created: the Cavendish, a large white-stucco, fifty-six-unit building on Columbia Road at 1628, built by Harry Wardman and designed by A.H. Beers (it is now demolished); and at 1664, a four-story apartment house also of white stucco. Just to the south, at 2551 Seventeenth Street, there is a large, attractive four-story Classical Revival apartment house, built in 1917 by John L. Warren and also designed by Hunter and Bell. This is now a retirement building named Sarah's Circle.

Also on Columbia Road, at number 1658, is the Potter's House, a noted coffeehouse and bookstore that opened in 1960 as a beatnik-inspired avant-garde café. Much of the rest of the thoroughfare's south side was (and is) composed of two- and three-story commercial structures, in a variety of styles that were erected in the early 1900s, mainly with rental apartments above the first-floor retail spaces. These shops were typical of the time: tailors, card shops, small grocery stores, and the like. With Washington generally almost always having a portion of its population on the move, the apartments there appear to have always been in demand, and thus useful neighborhood components.

All Souls Church on Sixteenth Street at Harvard Street. *Photo by the author.*

Inside the Neighborhood

Farther down within the subdivision, a mix of housing was built, from middle class to working class. To the south, groups of basic but modern row houses were built around 1910 for the average working-class citizens, filling the streets along Kalorama Road and Champlain Street. The people moving there were not only some of the supporting employees for the wealthy who lived on Sixteenth Street, but also many of the individuals engaged in the work necessary to maintain the city itself—plumbers, electricians and service workers. These row houses were usually simple and not overly large, but solid and more than just adequate. And on Seventeenth Street—this being the segregated Washington of 1910—several medium-sized apartment buildings were constructed just for African American families. In some locations, such as on Florida Avenue on the area's southern side, other African Americans also had homes. In addition, up the hill near Columbia Road, some larger more upscale middle-class homes were built, with finer details. These were often sold to some of the many civil service government employees then living in the city.

When the area was first built out as it now exists, it held a range of people, both white and black residents, but during the mid-century era of desegregation, when all citizens were allowed to equally share civic resources, many of the neighborhood's whites left. Since the 1970s, however, a variety of individuals, including whites with healthier social values, have been moving back into the city and to this area; thus, the neighborhood of today is a mix of people and cultures, with a resulting mix of interests and aspirations. And additionally, beginning largely after 1970, a number of the Hispanic immigrants coming to the District have also made their homes in this area. For years, Adams Morgan proudly has been well known for its broad range of cultures.

With the turbulence of the 1960s having an effect on all of the District, a period of stagnation occurred in this area, with some increased crime and some civic decay; a number of local properties became neglected. But the situation would gradually improve. In the later part of the twentieth century, there came renewed interest in living in the city, and a fair amount of development took place in the area—with new construction such as Euclid Mews at Seventeenth and Euclid Streets, a twenty-four-unit townhouse condo project completed in 1980. In addition, a number of apartment buildings that had been built largely during the 1910s and 1920s were renovated and converted into either condos or co-ops. At 1654 Euclid Street, a mid-rise

Rowhouses along Ontario Road south of Euclid Street in 1949. *Historical Society of Washington, D.C., John P. Wymer Photograph Collection.*

The roller-skating rink on Kalorama Road at Seventeenth Street in 1949. *Historical Society of Washington, D.C., John P. Wymer Photograph Collection.*

upscale condo building, named Lot 33, was built as an all-new construction project in 2007.

In 1947, at the corner of Kalorama Road and Seventeenth Street, a large, sturdy, concrete-framed domed structure was built and opened as the National Arena, a roller rink and bowling alley. It also hosted wrestling matches, roller derbies, and later, rock concerts. In 1986, it became the Citadel Motion Picture Center, where portions of *Gardens of Stone* and other movies were filmed. In 2009, the building was renovated and Harris Teeter opened a modern, stylish supermarket in response to the demand created by new residents in the area. More information about the current and ongoing growth in the neighborhood is reviewed in the later chapter on activity in the twenty-first century.

***

A closer look at the social fabric that existed earlier in this "typically Washington" residential area of the old estate brings forward a couple points about the lives of its citizens. First, locally the old segregated society was rather polite—this being the nation's capital, of course. And there were those who wanted to show that segregation was civilized, which, of course, did not make this immoral system any better. Second, when this callous practice of segregation was finally lifted, the African American community sometimes displayed a justifiable unhappiness, especially when making attempts at reasonable integration; but very often, their efforts at equality were for a time unproductive. And a bit surprisingly, it appears that on occasion, a few blacks pushed ideas that were aimed at preserving some aspects of the earlier bad past. Thus, an examination now into the history of the neighborhood leads to the following observations about how society might possibly move beyond the lingering legacy of a segregated community.

Coming from a Divided Society and Looking Toward the Future

In this area, before the 1950s, whites and blacks lived quite closely together, but in separate spheres. The use of the mental partition that permitted this behavior was a holdover from the old days of slavery, and was doable, but not healthy. First and foremost, it was not fair. And with a bit of thinking, it became clear that this would not work over the long term, especially if each community, and the nation as a whole, expected to sensibly and ethically advance. But within this area's early twentieth-century expansion, with this segregation still in place, African Americans developed their own internal world, and their own small local village. A small but nice church, Meridian Hill Baptist (now named King Emmanuel Baptist Church), was erected in 1936 on the northwest corner of Ontario and Kalorama Roads, and a few neighborhood stores for blacks opened. How this local world was impacted and changed by the desegregation that followed—and how it continues to evolve within the present day—is not that often directly discussed, and is something that is not yet really resolved, here, or nationally, wherever it exists. In fact, this is an example of a matter that is today in discussion worldwide, as the modern world continues to envelop and subsume many of the smaller cultures of various locales.

This is a somewhat complicated issue to take up and examine. How can one effectively keep one's own distinct culture and history, without losing it when it becomes absorbed into the larger society's dominant ethos? And then there follows the next question: if—and after—one has succeeded at retaining one's ethnicity, just how is it possible to still comfortably and smoothly live—socially, productively and happily—in the country's larger cultural ocean? For a time, some African Americans here, and elsewhere, promoted a black-only objective for the District of Columbia; some still do today. But of course, this does not work, any more than having some other group claim the city. Not too long ago, the general U.S. culture was almost exclusively the white one, and in some respects, it still continues to be. But increasingly, with what has happened in today's world, the pervading culture that is seen most everywhere now is a broad mix of almost all groups, and more and more, this "culture" is becoming a world of technology, with few true ethnic ties to any one group, except perhaps as window-dressing. And so it appears that in the future—and even today—in most urban locations, the core elements of each group's culture will need to be artificially and deliberately maintained—if that culture is still wanted.

The Builders

The developers, the property owners, the builders, and the architects who created the houses and apartment buildings that sit inside the subdivision were, for the most part, local District people. Typically, they were small-scale builders who likely worked with the same sets of people on projects throughout the areas of the District then being developed. Noted and prolific D.C. developer Harry Wardman also had his hand in the area, building a couple of mid-sized apartment houses, such as the one at 2426 Seventeenth Street, plus a number of nice row houses as well, including ones in the 2400 block of Ontario Road and on Seventeenth Street.

The costs of the homes then being sold, largely all of which were row houses, varied when new, from the lower amounts of $1,500 to $3,000 for the simpler working-class homes along Kalorama Road, up to the range of from $5,000 to $7,500 for the more elaborate ones, such as on Euclid Street and Columbia Road near Fifteenth Street. The upscale 1926 apartment building on Crescent Place was one of the early cooperatives in D.C.; its prices in 1926 were also upscale, the highest then for a D.C. co-op, from $6,000 to $29,000.

Here are a few representative examples of the homes, with construction information (costs shown here are usually what was planned and listed, and thus might often not be the actual, final cost):

- *In the 1700 block of Euclid Street: 1724 to 1732, a cluster of six row houses built in 1906. J.F. McCormick, owner; William C. Lewis, builder. N.T. Haller, architect. $6,000 each. McCormick developed several groups of row houses in the area, and Lewis (alone and with others) built many structures, house and buildings, in the nearby areas.*
- *1706 to 1710 Euclid: John Haislip, owner and builder; N.T. Haller, architect. Built in 1911. $3,200 each.*
- *1712 to 1722 Euclid: Built in 1912 by John Haislip, owner and builder; Edward Vollard, architect. $4,000 each.*
- *1717 to 1731 Euclid: J.F. McCormick, owner and builder; William Palmer, architect. Built in 1906. Eight row houses, $5,000 each.*
- *On Ontario, 2301 to 2323: George Rees, owner and builder, Hill & Randall, architects. Built in 1908. $2,400 each.*
- *At 2315 to 2323 Ontario: John L. Warren, owner; John Brennan, builder; Hunter & Bell, architects. Built in 1908. $3,000 each.*
- *On Kalorama Road: 1650 to 1682: 16 units, built in 1914 by D.J. Dunigan, owner, architect and builder. $1,600 each.*
- *At 2401 Ontario Road: A 22 unit apartment building. Edmund Warder, owner and builder; George T. Santmyers, architect. Built 1943.*
- *At 2303 & 2305 Seventeenth Street: Row houses, Margaret Ogle owner; J.H. McIntyre, builder. Built in 1906. $3,000 each.*
- *At 1501 to 1505 Harvard Street: Built in 1914 for William Moreland, owner; Upton-Smoot, builder; Donn & Deming, architects. $4,500 each.*

- *On Ontario: 2300 to 2322: A cluster of row houses. Built in 1907 by M.J. Keane, owner and builder; John Miller, architect. $2,500 each.*
- *On Ontario: 2429 to 2437: Five row houses built in 1913; Harry Wardman, owner and builder; Frank Russell White, architect. $3,200 each.*
- *At 2370 Champlain Street: A 32 unit apartment building; G.G..Loehler, owner and builder; Claughton West, architect. Built in 1926.*
- *At 2501 to 215 Seventeenth Street are eight more Harry Wardman row houses, built in 1904 and designed by Nicholas R. Grimm. $4,000 each.*

With the modern changes in construction that occurred a little before 1900, home building became much easier and more efficient to do, thus also reducing costs. The ready availability of well-milled lumber and the use of power equipment made the work proceed not only more quickly and with fewer complications, but also allowed the workers to do a better job. The introduction of portable electric power tools had a major impact on the quality and detailing of the finished homes. The craft workers creating these structures seem to have learned quickly to do a quality job, and then moved from project to project. Similarities of style and detail appear again and again in the finished homes of the different developers, and most often, this detailing aspired to emulate the better work of the older handcrafted homes of the wealthy.

The city infrastructure that was needed on the inside local streets—the curbs, sidewalks and, proper paving—generally followed the home building, and evidently was done only as it became necessary. The city, of course, set out regulations for development, with the city's civil engineers first properly constructing the area's arterial roads.

Home Prices over the Years

Generally, within the subdivision, as with most of the city, home prices over time slowly but steadily grew, with the expected dips and rises, until the era of desegregation. Then prices dropped when, unfortunately, many white D.C. residents became uneasy, moving away to the suburbs; this urban decline continued during the 1960s and into the 1970s, bringing prices for owner-occupied homes down further—also occurring in some other parts of the city. Many of the neighborhood's properties decayed or were converted, often carelessly, into multi-unit rentals. Some of these homes were also then purchased for low prices by young, adventurous people, perhaps even by hippie types, who then either restored them or, in some cases, ruined the houses through inept or careless behavior. Others were purchased by less well-off families. The rise in housing prices over the next thirty years is well documented, and most of the local previously depressed properties are now worth many times their earlier low prices. Housing values in this area have continued to rise, with the 2008 housing slump having had an adverse impact, but certainly not the problem seen in some other locations. Prices have risen in part because this area continues to be a very desirable spot in which to live. Broadly, the increased values are seen to be a good thing. Today, however, the issue of high housing prices, coupled with the growing unavailability of good employment, together highlight an increasing mismatch with the reality of living in the United States. How to effectively deal with this situation is a serious question for citizens and for civic groups, locally and nationally.

The Residents

And what of the residents: the people living in the areas of the subdivision? Initially, most of the houses were purchased and then owner-occupied; over the years, the residents became a mix of owners and renters. Our modern world—since 1900—has created a stable and reliable recording-keeping system that allows most anyone today to find the basic information of many of the people who have lived in this area. Individual family stories are also sometimes in the records, so it is important that the core databases be maintained. A number of interesting oral histories have been produced in the recent past, with some of these records being archived at local Washington, D.C. historical libraries.

INDUSTRIAL

Also inside the subdivision—at its southwest corner on Champlain Street just above Florida Avenue—there is a Pepco electric substation that was built in 1930 to handle the area's increasing energy needs; it is not far from the site of the area's first electric powerhouse, a small dynamo built in 1892 on Ontario just above Kalorama. (This dynamo, an early generator of electricity, was built by the Rock Creek Railway Co. to help power its new electric streetcars. A street test area was first set up on nearby Florida Avenue, with the new line then being built to run up Eighteenth Street and then out to Chevy

Chase, Maryland.) So after 1930, some further light industrial development occurred nearby, partially in areas that had previously contained some of the older nineteenth-century and largely African American–occupied homes—a number of which were torn down after being judged to be substandard, with the residents then being displaced. In the mid-twentieth century, without much civic consideration, this type of small-scale, ad hoc redevelopment was also occurring in several other parts of the city.

Automobiles. At 1781 Florida Avenue, at the very corner of the old estate, the sizeable Liberty Garage was built in 1921; in 1933, it was modified to become a popular Ford dealership named Cherner Motor Company and is now a multi-use building. This building had anchored the "car culture" of this area. Earlier, up on Champlain Street, a few other auto dealers, garages and repair shops had been set up as this newly devised form of travel had first come into use shortly after 1900. For example, at 2115 Champlain Street, a large service station had been constructed for electric automobiles, which were a popular form of city transportation prior to 1925. This location later continued on as a Studebaker dealership. Until recently, there were also a couple gasoline service stations on this street. Years earlier, horses had been stabled at the creek edge that ran along here, so this area evolved and developed as a logical spot for auto care, parking and sales.

Other types of industrial construction were also occurring. A large, nicely detailed six-story warehouse for the Security Storage Company was built in 1925 at 1701 on Florida Avenue (which by then had become a less-used, more local street), and during the middle of the twentieth century, some low-rise office buildings and storage facilities were built along Kalorama Road. Off of Seventeenth Street, a local printing company named Colortone Press also had its production plant; this building has since been renovated and adapted for new mixed uses, including housing.

Schools

The Marie H. Reed Learning Center sits on Champlain Street. In 1971, it replaced the old Thomas P. Morgan Elementary School, which, before it was torn down, stood right at the western edge of Meridian Hill's land, near Florida Avenue, on California Street between Champlain and Eighteenth Streets. The Morgan School (built in 1902) was the school for African American students in the unjust, segregated era. It was named for Thomas Morgan, who had been an active city leader and a district commissioner from 1879 to 1883. The replacement Learning Center was named for Bishop Marie Reed (1915–1969), a community activist, minister and civic leader. When it was built, this modern structure featured a number of neighborhood amenities such as a daycare center, tennis courts and a swimming pool, as well as the new school. There are plans now underway to remodel and update the center, which is currently showing signs of age.

H.D. Cooke Elementary School, at 2525 Seventeenth Street, is an attractive brick structure that was built in 1909, designed by architects William Marsh and Walter Peter. This school was renovated and improved in 2009, with a thoughtful emphasis on environmentally smart construction methods, and with active input and assistance from local residents. The school, well made and thoroughly modern when erected, was named for Henry D. Cooke (1825–1881), who had become the District's first governor after the D.C. government was reorganized by Congress in 1871; Cooke had served from 1871 to 1873. The school replaced an earlier structure—Victorian and stern-looking—that had been built in 1898, as the area was first beginning to blossom. This older building, nearby at 2428 Seventeenth Street, was later renamed the Morgan Annex and became a black school as part of the segregated education system. Today, this vintage school structure has been rehabilitated into condo apartments known as the Morgan Annex Lofts.

THE EASTERN SIDE

On the eastern side of the subdivision, not to be overlooked: To the east of the park, in the Fifteenth Street area—indeed a part of Meridian Hill—the land was also being developed; there, for example, several well-made mid-rise apartment houses were erected. Starting on the northern edge, at 1474 Columbia Road, there sits the Maycroft, a solid four-story middle-class apartment building constructed in 1922 by Isadore Freund and designed by architects Stern and Tomlinson. Just south of this building, on Fifteenth Street, are several more apartment houses in a variety of styles, including Hilltop House at 1475 Euclid Street, built in 1949. These buildings from the 1930s and 1940s, some plain, some elaborate, sit among a few of Mary Henderson's buildings. One attractive example at 2325 Fifteenth Street is Garden Towers, a seventy-five-unit,

Garden Towers at 2325 Fifteenth Street, built in 1937 and designed by George T. Santmyers. A typical building, but quietly contributing to the city. *Photo by the author.*

six-story brick building constructed in 1937 and designed by prolific D.C. architect George T. Santmyers. Farther south are a few small and generally high-quality apartment houses, along with several attractive row houses. Over at 2901 Sixteenth Street, in a prominent position, is the Copperfield, a six-story brick basic Classic Revival apartment house that was built in 1912 and designed by Claughton West; it is now a condominium building.

Architect George T. Santmyers designed a remarkably large number of row houses and many apartment buildings in the District, in a variety of motifs, including Deco, Gothic, Moderne, and the simpler International style. Working with many developers, and often having to work within a strict budget, he gave the city many fine structures that continue to contribute to the visual fabric that is seen every day. The extra pieces of detailing that he adroitly worked into his designs often just sit quietly in the background of city scenes, but are welcome attractive neighborhood components. When he was allowed to do something extra, his works, such as the large apartment building at 3901 Connecticut Avenue (in the Cleveland Park area), are truly beautiful creations. The citizens of Washington really do owe George Santmyers more recognition.

Back at Fifteenth Street, along the named horizontal streets, such as Harvard, some typical solid two- and three-story row houses were also created, mainly from 1910 to 1914. This area, now part of Columbia Heights, was developed along with the general growth of middle-class housing then occurring citywide, with the typical standard, but good generic detailing. On the south side of Columbia Road is a stretch of some larger, well-constructed and more upscale row houses, built in 1905; for example, that same year, a large corner house, costing a pricey $12,000, was erected at 1500 Columbia Road.

MODERN AREA NEIGHBORHOODS

Most of the area of the old Meridian Hill estate became part of Adams Morgan, a neighborhood whose name was formed in 1958 by local residents working to integrate, in a progressive manner, the two major area elementary schools: the all-white John Quincy Adams School, which was (and still is) over on Nineteenth Street, and the all-black Thomas P. Morgan School on the west side of Champlain Street. The community of Adams Morgan, located east of Rock Creek and north of the original city, has become world famous as a vibrant, eclectic and progressive neighborhood, and a good place to live, too.

The intersection of Sixteenth Street with Florida Avenue is the meeting point of three major city neighborhoods: Adams Morgan to the west, Columbia Heights to the northeast, and Shaw to the southeast. Sixteenth Street, the divider between Adams Morgan and Columbia Heights, cuts through the old estate's land. The Columbia Heights subdivision was laid out not long after Meridian Hill's plan was created, and takes its name, in general, from the Columbia College property—but even from its initial proposal, the neighborhood's area extended more broadly to the north and the east. Thus, Columbia Heights also encompassed some of the land then still owned by the Holmead family, plus the land from a few of the estates and farms that had been established around the time of Washington's creation. One such estate was the noted William J. Stone property, just across from Columbia College on the east side of Fourteenth Street.

And so Meridian Hill Park itself, and the small and medium-sized apartment buildings to the east along Fifteenth Street—along with Mary Henderson's elaborate concoctions also on that street—are a part of Columbia Heights. Many of these apartment houses, with their thoughtful architectural details and large, well-planned units, still retain their original layouts.

To further add to the mix, the modern properties situated on the south side of Columbia Road—at the upper edge of the old estate—face the Lanier Heights subdivision to the north, and in order to create a unified identity for this busy thoroughfare, they are usually considered to be part of Lanier Heights. In turn, Lanier Heights is normally considered to be part of the larger Adams Morgan.

Going south from Columbia Road, between Sixteenth and Eighteenth Streets, the western piece of the old estate is now known as Reed-Cooke, named for the two neighborhood schools there.

All the areas of Meridian Hill are within the 20009 zip code; in the organization of the District of Columbia government, Meridian Hill is a part of Ward One. The land of the subdivision is also spread among the following smaller citizen Advisory Neighborhood Commissions: 1B05, 1B06, 1B07, 1C06, 1C07 and 1C08.

***

As a neighborhood identifier, Meridian Hill's name is generally now only used in the area immediately surrounding Meridian Hill Park. Neighborhoods and their boundaries in Washington, as in many cities, are somewhat loosely defined. Thus, it often occurs that some D.C. city addresses can be said to exist—at the same time!—in two or even three separately named neighborhoods.

5

Mary Henderson

In the modern history of Meridian Hill, Mary Foote Henderson stands out as the most important personality of the area; she fundamentally shaped the look and the architecture of much of the neighborhood and was a key participant in the creation of Meridian Hill Park. Her long and active life was one with many remarkable facets.

Mary Foote was born on July 21, 1841, in Seneca Falls, New York, the daughter of Eunice Newton and Elisha Foote, a well-respected lawyer and judge; she was also the niece of Senator Samuel Foote of Connecticut. Interestingly, Elisha Foote was also a mathematician, and served as commissioner of the U.S. Patent Office during 1868 and 1869. Growing up, Mary received a comprehensive education at several schools, including what is now Skidmore College in New York and then later at Washington University in St. Louis. She was fluent in French and had a lifelong interest in the nature of society and philosophy and in the visual arts.

In 1868, Mary Foote wed Missouri senator John B. Henderson, who had co-authored the Thirteenth Amendment to the Constitution—the amendment that abolished slavery in 1865. John, a friend and supporter of Abraham Lincoln, retired from the Senate in 1869, and he and Mary then returned to Missouri. There, through some shrewd—and some timely—bond investments made by John, the Hendersons became quite wealthy. Mary had one surviving child, a son named John Jr. While she lived in St. Louis, Mary worked on many projects in the art world, and was active in promoting the issue of voting rights for women, becoming the president of the Missouri State Suffrage Association. In 1887, John and Mary permanently returned to the District of Columbia.

Mary Foote Henderson in 1913. *Library of Congress.*

Henderson Castle

The couple then bought up dozens of real estate lots just outside the original northern boundary of the city, in the Meridian Hill subdivision. Beginning in 1888, on the large bluff that rose beyond the northwest corner of Sixteenth Street and Florida Avenue, the Hendersons constructed a grand brownstone mansion, initially costing $50,000 and designed by New England architect Eugene C. Gardner, author of the progressive 1875 book *Homes and How to Make Them*. Their mansion famously became known as Henderson's Castle (and earlier also sometimes as Boundary Castle). This rambling structure was indeed built to look like a castle, with crenellated walls and a huge triple-arched stone entranceway. Architect Gardner had first trained as a stonemason and thus was well versed in the intricacies of working in the heavy Romanesque Revival style used here; among his various commissions were a number of massive public buildings such as railroad stations and hospitals. When looking at his work, it is clearly obvious that he was comfortable and assured when

Henderson Castle about 1920, on Sixteenth Street. Note the newly built Meridian Mansions apartments to the north. *MLK D.C. Public Library, Washingtoniana Collection.*

working with stone and brick. The reddish-brown Seneca sandstone that he chose for the home was also used to construct an impressive fortified retaining wall along Sixteenth Street, with entrance gates at the driveway going up to the mansion. Inside the imposing edifice, there was a large ballroom for entertaining, which the Hendersons often did. Taking advantage of the dramatic view from its location on the side of the hill, the house faced south toward the Potomac. For several years, the Hendersons continued tinkering with their home, adding more pieces onto it.

The *Evening Star* newspaper reported on the first dinner held at the new home on February 10, 1890. Here are two excerpts:

> Boundary castle, the superb home of ex-Senator and Mrs. Jno B. Henderson of Missouri, was thrown open last night for the first time to a large company, the guests of honor being the delegates to the international American congress (later becoming the Pan American Union), of which the host is a member. This new home, recently completed, is situated at the head of 16th street…Mr. Henderson's house is modeled on the style of a Normandy castle…It has square towers and rounded recesses, balconies, porticos and archways of stone.
>
> ***
>
> Mrs. Henderson is slight, petite and blonde, and being bright and vivacious in manner is a charming hostess of her magnificent surroundings. Mr. Jno. B. Henderson, Jr., who is in his junior year at Harvard, was present, assisting his parents to extend the hospitalities of the castle.

Mary Henderson's interest in the nearby neighborhood, and her enthusiasm for the City Beautiful movement of the early twentieth century, helped to ultimately lead to the construction of the beautifully crafted terraced park on Sixteenth Street. As the wife of a former U.S. senator, and with a large cache of money, Mary was in a fairly rare position of power, which enabled her to plan and then actually fashion her focused concept of what the area could become.

A visionary, a health enthusiast and a social activist, Mary was determined to make Meridian Hill the gateway to the nation's capital, and poured her energies into accomplishing this goal. She also realized that she might possibly also make a good amount of money buying and selling land in the area, and in doing so, could control the type of development that would take place there. So on a number of the real estate parcels that the Hendersons had purchased, Mary constructed elaborate residences, which she then sold as embassies and legations. The architect George Oakley Totten Jr., working with Mary, designed nearly a dozen of these buildings on Fifteenth and Sixteenth Streets as part of her plan to create a diplomatic enclave in the Meridian Hill area. And not far from her building activity, in 1924 she provided the land on Sixteenth Street at Lamont Street for the planned Mount Pleasant Library, today a local landmark.

Although Mary is most closely associated with the area's development, her husband, John, a lawyer, was also very much involved in some of the real estate projects. For example, in 1905, he was part of a group that worked on the financing, planning and construction of the large and noteworthy Kennesaw apartment house, located at 3060 Sixteenth Street in the Mount Pleasant neighborhood, just north of Meridian Hill. John also spent time working with local and national economic development groups; he was so well regarded that he was chosen to serve as a regent of the Smithsonian Institution. John was born in Virginia in 1826, later moving to Missouri as a child; he passed away in the District in 1913.

With an active interest in civic improvement, Mary frequently lobbied Congress with proposals for a number of projects that she considered beneficial to the Meridian Hill area. Just before 1900, and supporting the ideas of urban planner Franklin W. Smith, Mary proposed construction of a colossal presidential mansion on Meridian Hill to replace the White House. But obviously, this plan gained little support.

In 1911, largely because of Mary Henderson's ongoing lobbying efforts, Meridian Hill was considered as a possible site for the construction of the memorial to Abraham Lincoln. John Russell Pope, who also designed the Temple of the Scottish Rite and the Abraham Lincoln birthplace memorial, prepared designs for the memorial. Pope proposed a huge edifice recalling the mausoleum at Halicarnassus (an imposing creation that he admired), which would have straddled Sixteenth Street, but this design was rejected by the U.S. Commission of Fine Arts because the size and majesty of the structure did not fit in with the residential character of the surrounding area. Even after the commission rejected Meridian Hill as a site for the Lincoln Memorial, Mrs. Henderson petitioned Congress in 1912 with another design for the memorial, which she had commissioned from Frederick Murphy and W.B. Olmsted. This design was also rejected.

One of Mrs. Henderson's more famous—or infamous—crusades was to change the name of Sixteenth Street to "Avenue of the Presidents" and line the street with busts of all the presidents and vice presidents of the United

Senator John B. Henderson. *Library of Congress.*

States. While she actually succeeded in having legislation passed to change the name of the street in 1913, the Commission of Fine Arts denied her request to construct the busts. One year later, after the name "Avenue of the Presidents" proved to be unpopular locally, Sixteenth Street's original name was restored.

The Senate's important McMillan Plan of 1901 proposed major changes to Washington's civic appearance. After the Senate had decided to accept the plan's recommendation that a large public park be created on Meridian Hill, Mary actively assisted with the park's planning. And later, on a number of occasions, she was successful in persuading Congress to appropriate funds so that work on the park could continue. Following her death in 1931, the Commission of Fine Arts praised her efforts on behalf of Meridian Hill and stated in a report: "Persistently she labored during four decades, persuading and convincing Senators and Representatives; single-handed and alone she appeared before committees of Congress to urge approval for the work of development. She won."

Mary Henderson also had some success with writing, creating several books, including *Practical Cooking and Dinner Giving*—a treatise on entertaining, sometimes used as a reference guide for learning proper etiquette. Mary also became a strong advocate for temperance and vegetarianism, writing a book on health and diet called *The Aristocracy of Health.* She famously hosted vegetarian dinners and sponsored advocates of yoga. Her crusading activities in support of temperance became well known. Mary joined with a group that publicly lobbied for the prohibition of alcohol, and in 1906, allowed members of this group to empty out—into the street—her husband's well-stocked wine cellar. This event was well reported in the city's newspapers; her activities were often covered by the press. Thereafter, all of the Henderson parties were alcohol-free.

Mary's approaches to her life and to her activities were together a true study of contradictions. She was progressive and reactionary; she was generous and selfish; she was a freethinker and also frostily autocratic. Her husband co-wrote the amendment abolishing slavery, and yet she later helped to displace a small community of freed blacks when implementing her construction plans. As she grew older, she apparently became more rigidly set in her belief in the correctness of disciplined living.

In her defense, it should be remembered that Mary was very much a product of her time, and while sometimes callous, she was most often working for the civic good—single-mindedly, to be sure, and as she saw it, of course. In the end, what she accomplished was very beneficial to not only Washington, but also the country as a whole. Her diplomatic connections with some of the most-developed nations of the world were a part of the larger series of relationships occurring in this country as the United States moved to become a major economic and cultural force in the rapidly changing world.

Mary died at nearly age ninety on July 16, 1931, and after her will was read, major legal wrangling over the distribution of her estate ensued. Mary had willed $200,000 and a mansion to her Japanese secretary, Jesse Shima, and much of the rest to Battle Creek College, but left nothing to her only close relative, Mrs. Beatrice Henderson Wholean, the adopted daughter of her son—there had been a serious falling out between to two women. The will was immediately contested in court. So, during this time of legal challenge in the mid-1930s, the castle was leased to a private social club and, ironically, then became an after-hours "bottle" nightclub, and later a rooming house. The neighbors to the north, up on Crescent Place, Eugene and Agnes Meyer, who at the time were the owners of the *Washington Post*, got tired of the noise that was being generated and bought the property. After that, the castle was used for a short period as a school before it was finally torn down in 1949, with only the great stone wall and entrance gate turrets surviving the wrecking ball. Several uses were later proposed for the site, but nothing occurred until 1977, when developer Lawrence Brandt built the Beekman Place community of condominium townhouses on the land.

MARY'S PROJECTS

The well-crafted structures that Mary Henderson and architect George Oakley Totten Jr. built on Meridian Hill have very definitely contributed to the good visual appearance of Washington.

George Oakley Totten Jr. (1866–1939) was born in New York City and was an 1892 graduate of Columbia University's School of Architecture; during the following two years, he studied at the École des Beaux-Arts in Paris, receiving a classical training. In 1896, he became the chief designer in the Architect's Office of the U.S. Treasury Department, where he likely learned of the best methods of doing quality modern construction. He was there until 1898, when he left to establish a private practice in the District, becoming a fashionable architect to the wealthy. He is best known for his richly ornamented mansions and embassies in Washington, as well as for executing some other civil and private commissions in the eastern United States. After doing some work for Mary at her castle in the early 1900s (she was occasionally adding on to the castle compound), George became her collaborator, shaping most of her larger architectural projects.

These striking, substantial, and well-detailed creations have been used as embassies, homes, headquarters for agencies of the federal government and occasionally as headquarters for independent organizations. Here is a list of most of the major buildings that Henderson and Totten crafted, along with brief descriptions:

2600 Sixteenth Street

This was the first building to be constructed by Mary and was known as the Pink Palace; it was built in 1905 in the Venetian Gothic/ Renaissance style. Originally a private residence, this large and elaborate creation was first occupied by Oscar Straus, secretary of commerce in the cabinet of President Theodore Roosevelt. After several different owners and uses, it

The Pink Palace at 2600 Sixteenth Street, shown circa 1915–20. *Historical Society of Washington, D.C.*

became home to the Inter-American Defense Board, which today continues to have its headquarters there.

2460 Sixteenth Street

2460 Sixteenth Street, formerly the French Embassy, seen in 1915. *Historical Society of Washington, D.C.*

Built in 1907 and then leased to the French for use as their embassy, this stately stone Beaux Arts mansion was designed with some well-wrought architectural details; the George A. Fuller Co. was the builder. It now houses the Council for Professional Recognition, a nonprofit educational association.

2622 Sixteenth Street

Created in the Spanish Renaissance style, this three-story limestone structure with good detailing, and with a five-story tower, is now the Embassy of Lithuania, which it has been since 1926. When it was constructed in 1909, this building had a companion structure, which unfortunately was torn down and replaced in 1965 by a rather bland nine-story apartment house.

A building detail of the Embassy of Lithuania at 2622 Sixteenth Street. *Photo by the author.*

2640 Sixteenth Street

This handsome three-bay limestone edifice, in the French style with a Mansard roof, was built in 1910. It was purchased by Poland in 1919 for diplomatic use, and today this fine building continues to serve as the home of the Embassy of Poland.

2633 Fifteenth Street

Meridian Hill Studios, a two-story stucco-clad structure, was built in 1922 as a thirteen-unit apartment complex for artists. An early cooperative, it began as the Meridian Hill Club. It was noted for the ceramic mantels designed by Totten's wife, sculptor Vicken von Post Totten, and additionally has some nice Arts & Crafts–style touches. It continues today as a housing co-op.

2801 Sixteenth Street

Mary Henderson built this marvelous creation in 1922 as a possible vice-presidential residence, but this impressive, finely detailed structure was never accepted by the U.S. government because it was considered too grand an edifice and too costly to maintain. (It was also initially mildly criticized for being a rather eclectic mix of styles inside.) Built by

2801 Sixteenth Street not long after it was built. For many years it was the Embassy of Spain. *Historical Society of Washington, D.C.*

the William P. Lipscomb Construction Company, the property was later purchased by Spain for use as its embassy, which it was for many years. While owned by Spain, the property was further improved with new structures in the rear, and with additional interior detailing. It is now serving as a Spanish Cultural Center.

2535 Fifteenth Street

At the corner with Euclid Street, this imposing five-story Beaux Arts building sits on land that was sold to the Netherlands in 1922. In conjunction with Totten, the Netherlands government had this structure designed and built as its embassy. It is today home to the Embassy of Ecuador.

2401 Fifteenth Street (Meridian Hall)

This solid and proper 1923 stone Tudor Revival–style mansion served for a time as the Egyptian legation. At present, the national center of the Art of Living Foundation is located there.

Meridian Hall at 2401 Fifteenth Street. *Photo by the author.*

2437 Fifteenth Street

Built in 1928, this three-story Italian Renaissance–style mansion was formerly the Brazilian embassy. The last of Mary's buildings, it has an attractive stucco exterior with a red tile roof. Now known as the Josephine Butler Parks Center, it is home to the local nonprofit civic association Washington Parks and People.

2437 Fifteenth Street, built in 1928. *Photo by the author.*

***

This is just a selected overview of the remarkable pieces of architecture that were created around Meridian Hill. Many other reference sources, such as books and articles—some general, some with specific subjects—can be found at libraries, in book stores and online. With a bit of hunting—which can be fun—one can indeed find some thoughtful in-depth reviews and evaluations of the neighborhood's exceptional buildings.

6

Meridian Hill Park

The following account of the park, a major component of modern-day Meridian Hill's identity, is a general overview of this special piece of the landscape of the nation's capital.

Meridian Hill Park, an extraordinary and well-regarded civic creation, is located just north of Florida Avenue, between Fifteenth and Sixteenth Streets. On the park's northern side, it extends to Euclid Street; its boundary on the south is W Street, slightly displacing Florida Avenue. The twelve-acre park, in the style of an Italian garden, is a visually attractive and well-planned work of urban art that offers a pleasant setting for the people of Washington to visit and enjoy.

Sitting due north of the White House, the park takes its name, of course, from the early proposal to establish a national prime meridian for navigation and map-making purposes directly on the longitude of the White House. A plaque at the park's mid-point entrance on Sixteenth Street takes note of the 1804 stone meridian marker, which stood along this proposed meridian line (this was the Jefferson marker that sat next to Commodore Porter's home).

Designed and built between 1912 and 1936, Meridian Hill Park has been under the jurisdiction of the National Park Service since 1933. The idea of a park at the site was put forward in the 1901 McMillan Plan for the city, which originally suggested a larger park on both sides of Sixteenth Street to showcase the site's panoramic views and important position relative to the L'Enfant plan for the city. In the end, the plan's civic engineers decided, with Mary Henderson's input, that a smaller—but finely crafted—park was more appropriate. As ultimately built, the multi-structured park was divided into two principal areas: the lower park, with a water cascade of linked basins, symmetrical stairways and a large reflecting pool surrounded by a plaza, and the upper park, with an open mall, wooded areas flanking the mall and a broad terrace overlooking the lower park. Overall, the vertical rise within the park—from its lowest point to its highest—is about seventy-five feet.

In 1901, the Senate Park Commission, with its McMillan plan, laid out a proposed set of formal changes to Washington's civic appearance, most famously planning to reconfigure the city's National Mall. After this commission had decided, with more input from Mary, that a park on Meridian Hill was a good idea, planning for its creation slowly proceeded through the government's many offices. Mary—strong-willed, intelligent, vigorous and well connected—very much championed the park. Later, throughout the many years of park construction, she lobbied Congress to maintain the flow of funding necessary to complete the project.

By an act of Congress on June 25, 1910, Meridian Hill Park was established. The federal government also purchased the land for the park in 1910 and began planning for its construction in 1912. The first official plans for the park were drawn up by landscape architect George Burnap and approved by the U.S. Commission of Fine Arts in early 1914, with the construction work commencing shortly thereafter. Burnap's walled Neoclassical design fit well with the steep topography and exploited the views from the crest of the hillside. The key features of his layout were centered on a single longitudinal axis extending north–south through the site. On the elevated north end of the park, he proposed a fountain, formal gardens and a great terrace. The dramatic water cascade of linked basins was planned for the steep slope to the south, ending in rectangular reflecting pools on a plaza at the foot of the hill. In 1917, landscape architect Horace Peaslee replaced Burnap but remained generally true to Burnap's intentions. Peaslee, however, abandoned most of the elaborate gardens of the upper portion of the park and replaced them with an open mall; over the years, this mall has been a well-used part of the park.

As conceived by the two architects, the plan was a highly structured composition and involved the creative skills of many people. The park's actual ground-planting scheme was designed by the New York firm of landscape architects Vitale, Brinckerhoff and Geiffert. Ferruccio Vitale was a talented and well-respected creator of large, planned garden spaces throughout the eastern United States. And happily, as the National Park Service has noted about the park: in the past, gardens of this size and detail were generally reserved for aristocrats, but Meridian Hill Park, a product of democracy, was made for all people.

Meridian Hill Park under construction. *Library of Congress.*

The construction of the park relied on techniques and materials that were used in a deliberate and particular manner. Almost all of the structural elements in this highly organized landscape—the terraces, walls, and pavements—were rendered in precast and cast-in-place concrete, treated with special care. The concrete contractor, John J. Earley, was a truly skilled craftsman who interpreted mosaic pavements, urns, balustrades, niches and planting containers with a carefully formulated concrete. Meridian Hill Park is unique in that it served as a laboratory for this experimentation with this new medium of construction—concrete aggregate. Concrete aggregate consists of small pebbles specially selected for size and color that are added to the concrete; the construction forms are then pulled while the surface is still not completely set. Wire-brushing and acid-washing are then used to expose the pebbles to create the texture for the finished appearance. In the early years of construction, several test areas were built at the site before the park's final look and shape were established. John Early and his band of craftsmen then worked for years on the creation of the park.

The works of art situated within the park are an integral part of its overall design. Since the 1920s, several notable monuments and memorials have been created for the park's landscape, and have often been installed with much ceremony. The Buchanan Memorial, crafted by sculptor Hans Schuler, working with architect William G. Beecher, was one of the first planned for the park, although it was not dedicated at its location until 1930. This imposing, well-detailed creation is the only memorial to President James Buchanan in Washington today. And a statue of Joan of Arc, a copy of the figure created by Paul Dubois at Reims Cathedral, was installed in 1922, directly on the main cross-axis of the park. A large and stately sculpture of

Statue of Joan of Arc, erected in 1922. This is a copy of the figure by Paul Dubois at Reims Cathedral. *Photo by the author.*

Meridian Hill Park: the Lower Cascade today. *Photo by the author.*

Dante, by sculptor Ettore Ximenes, was also put in place that same year. And a finely made marble allegorical figure of Serenity, the work of sculptor Jose Clara, was installed in 1925.

With its dramatic design, Meridian Hill Park stands out as a bold undertaking: the idea of creating a Renaissance villa landscape in the middle of an American city to serve as a public park and cultural institution is indeed special. The park may be one of the most successful examples of Neoclassical park design in the United States, and is a remarkable work, involving the creative talents of many fine craftworkers and artists. Along Sixteenth Street, especially when looking from the south, the park's notably cohesive appearance and high order of craftsmanship are clearly apparent. Its overall integrity and the masterful sureness of its plan and construction single it out for recognition.

***

Following its official dedication in 1936, the park became a popular recreational spot for open-air concerts and stage performances, and was a much-visited neighborhood destination. By the 1960s, however, the park had begun to show some age, and with many residents leaving the city for the suburbs, the park became less used and began to decline. Crime and some drug dealing then became serious problems there. With so many social concerns having arisen at that time, the government's resources were stretched, and park maintenance suffered.

After a political rally held at the park in 1969, a movement was begun to rename the entire park Malcolm X Park, in honor of the political activist. Ultimately however, after discussion and review, Congress did not permit this controversial name change. Today, the name Meridian Hill Park remains its official designation and is the name generally used by neighborhood residents and people throughout the D.C. region when referring to the park. But a few in the city still choose to use the name Malcolm X Park.

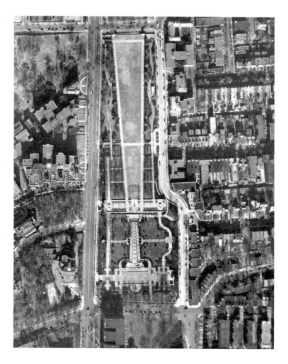

Aerial view of the park, taken about 1936, with the park essentially completed, and with Henderson Castle still present. *National Park Service.*

In 1990, with a general revitalization occurring in the surrounding neighborhood, a group of local citizens formed the Friends of Meridian Hill to help the park. This group, which later became Washington Parks and People, formed a citizens' crime patrol, spending many hours providing volunteer labor and doing grass-roots advocacy; this led to an award-winning partnership between the Friends and the National Park Service. The results were dramatic, with an impressive and welcome reduction in crime. As further proof of the renewed appreciation of the site, the park was placed on the National Register of Historic Places in 1994. In addition, new appropriations were provided by Congress to do restoration work on the park and to even rebuild some portions of it.

Starting in 2003, the first phase of this planned renovation work began, taking place primarily on the park's lower level, and involved the replacement of the park's eighty-year-old piping and electrical systems. These systems needed to be replaced in order for the fountains and electrical components in the park to function properly, especially in the park's striking major feature, the cascade. The work also included structural repairs to the park's historic concrete features: the walls, walkways and stairs. Benches on the upper level were also replaced. The second phase of restoration is now continuing and includes landscaping work, with irrigation and drainage construction. The upper-level playing fields and the lodge house have been rebuilt.

And so today, with a revitalized neighborhood, fresh citizen interest and participation, and ongoing renovations, Meridian Hill Park is now being renewed to again be a happily treasured part of Washington's exceptional park system.

7

A Present-Day Map of the Area

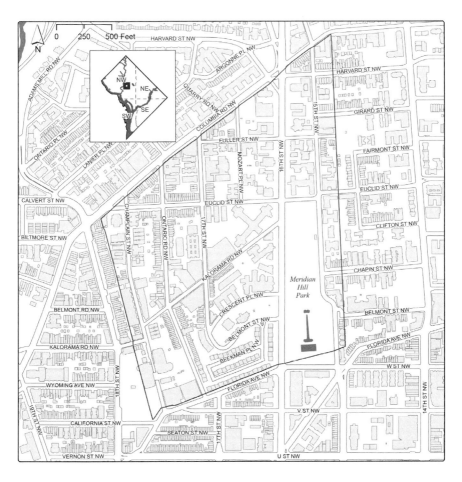

A map of the present-day Meridian Hill neighborhood, showing the outline of the original estate's property lines. *Map by Brian Kraft.*

Twenty-First Century:
The Neighborhood Today

Sixteenth Street

The area around Meridian Hill Park, which includes the prominent Sixteenth Street stretch of the neighborhood, continues to thrive. On each side of the park, the apartment buildings, both rental and owner-occupied, remain popular. For example, in 2014, the Dorchester House property was expanded along the Seventeenth Street side of its land, with new construction that created a building containing 117 additional apartments. At 2700 Sixteenth Street, there are plans now also underway—approved by the city—to thoughtfully and carefully convert the former Italian embassy building into condo apartments, with an attractive new structure being added onto the rear portion of its sizeable piece of land.

Meridian Hill Historic District

In March 2014, and after much good preparatory work by the city's Historic Preservation Office, the District of Columbia government approved the creation of the Meridian Hill Historic District. The city took this step after reviewing the area's qualifications and attributes—the factors that are necessary for the designation of such a district. After careful discussion, the Historic Preservation Review Board voted unanimously to formally approve the new district, thus making Meridian Hill the newest addition to the city's important and well-planned system of historic districts—areas that are now spread throughout Washington, D.C. The Meridian Hill Historic District covers the portion of the old Meridian Hill estate that contains the visually and historically noteworthy pieces of architecture deserving special recognition. The district is centered on Meridian Hill Park, encompassing the park and also including the finely detailed and significant buildings that exist on either side of the park, primarily on Fifteenth and Sixteenth Streets. Starting from V Street on the south, the district runs up to Columbia Road, and then goes a couple blocks farther north beyond this road to include a church and several apartment buildings of merit, which all help to contribute to the distinctive appearance of the neighborhood. This historic district will also bring some protection to these exceptional architectural creations that have helped to define Meridian Hill.

With its storied past and with the extraordinary architecture that today sits within this Historic District, the area is certainly worthy of such a designation.

REED-COOKE

By the early 1980s, the Reed-Cooke area of the old subdivision had evolved into a locale with its own identity; its name is taken from the neighborhood's two nearby schools—the Marie Reed Learning Center on Champlain Street, and the H.D. Cooke Elementary School on Seventeenth Street. Reed-Cooke, part of the larger Adams Morgan neighborhood, covers the area between Sixteenth and Eighteenth Streets, south of Columbia Road, down to Florida Avenue. Today, the area also supports a local citizen group, the Reed-Cooke Neighborhood Association.

Somewhat overlooked in the various studies of D.C. history, and on many maps, is the internal and less prominent land of the old estate. In some ways, this area might be the more genuine legacy of the farm; it contains all the basic components that make up a village: two true mansions, and a variety of other levels of housing, upscale and plain, both old and new; light industry, even a large warehouse; an electric substation, some retail stores and a couple nightclubs to fill out the locale. This inside area of the old subdivision is a mix of both professionals and the working class, with an African American community that dates to the latter part of the nineteenth century. Young tech-savvy workers have become residents. A number of Hispanic residents now also live in the neighborhood—originally drawn to the area by the proximity of the embassies of several Hispanic nations.

Today, with its desirable location, the area continues to attract people interested in city living and in the professional opportunities offered by the District; thus, there has been a considerable amount of recent new construction. Earlier, as the neighborhood developed over the years, a portion of Reed-Cooke adjacent to its residential sections also grew into an industrial area, and so a few businesses were established and warehouses were built, mostly along the southern edge near Florida Avenue.

As did much of central Washington, Reed-Cooke experienced a decline in the 1950s and 1960s. There was discussion at the time about possible actions that could be taken to remedy the situation. Some groups called for the removal of the area's small industrial section, along with clusters of the nearby houses. But other local residents then worked to stop this wholesale urban renewal, and steps were taken, with the city's assistance, to maintain affordable apartments in the area. Thus, with these efforts, the area now includes a mix of people with varying levels of income. A number of the small apartments buildings originally built mainly as working-class remain so today; into the later twentieth century, additional Hispanic residents moved into the area as rental housing became available in some of these buildings.

In the neighborhood today, Jubilee Housing, an offshoot of a local religious group, has several buildings with which it is providing subsidized housing and other types of social services for people in need. Jubilee also recently constructed an attractive multi-purpose conference center building at the corner of Mozart Place and Columbia Road, plus some older structures that were remodeled for its activities. It purchased its buildings beginning in the late 1970s. This is worthy work—providing housing and taking care of disadvantaged people—but there are competing issues in the city today. Thus, some neighbors pose the broader questions of what the ultimate goal is in continuing to provide such a general custodianship through multiple generations of families; how an artificial arrangement such as this can be maintained. And what this system, however well intentioned, is doing to these residents, and to the area. Some of the individuals being assisted have little interest in their neighborhood, or in contributing to it in a positive manner—bringing to mind the old adage that good neighbors make a good neighborhood. But the future is a fresh page.

As in many of the urban areas nationwide, this question of how the city should be utilized continues to be a matter of quiet contention in Reed-Cooke. The deepening national economic crisis will most likely change some aspects of this discussion. Additional local dialogue is also likely to occur, certainly a constructive step for the neighborhood's future.

The Reed-Cooke Overlay District

In the late 1980s, a number of local neighborhood groups and citizens, concerned about the growing potential for oversized large-scale development in the area, looked into ways of managing this issue. After a couple years of effort, in February 1991 the D.C. Zoning Office approved the creation of the Reed-Cooke Overlay District. (According to the zoning office, "overlay zoning is a regulatory tool that creates a special zoning district, placed over an existing base zone, which identifies special provisions in addition to those in the underlying base zone.") Regarding this overlay, the following is a description from the D.C. Zoning Office: "The Reed-Cooke Overlay District was established to protect existing housing and provide for the development of new housing, maintain heights and densities at appropriate levels, encourage small-scale business development that will not adversely affect the residential community [and] ensure that new nonresidential uses serve the local community." This overlay continues to be discussed, as Washington today works to deal with the changing world while still maintaining the city's historic fabric.

Meanwhile, and within this framework, since about the year 2000, a number of upscale new-construction housing projects have been executed locally along Champlain Street near Kalorama Road—a few as part of larger projects that generally front on Eighteenth Street. And then others along Kalorama Road itself, where some underutilized structures have also been remodeled, creating new homes. This adaptive reuse and conversion of several of the Reed-Cooke warehouses into condominiums, which has occurred mostly after 2005, and additional all-new construction of other condos, have worked to help revitalize the neighborhood. One such new development is the attractive, well-made Meridian Crescent, at 2200 Seventeenth Street, that was completed in 2006 at the southernmost corner of Seventeenth Street, taking advantage of the spectacular vista there, which inspired the original Meridian Hill. In general, the new construction is modern or stylized classic, but capably made and scaled to fit appropriately within the area. Some buildings have a postmodern design and add an agreeably dynamic element to the local street landscape. One such example is Adams Row, at 2301 Champlain Street, built in 2005 by the development firm of PN Hoffman.

Today's retail businesses and commercial activities in the area are a bit of an eclectic mix, ranging from the polished style of Harris Teeter's supermarket to tiny informal shops, often family-run, that cater to the neighborhood's diverse population. This includes a range of Hispanic food

Modern development at 2301 Champlain Street, at Kalorama Road, on a site that once held an auto service station. *Photo by the author.*

shops and restaurants. Most of the retail businesses are along Columbia Road, but other enterprises are scattered throughout the area, including some offices for professionals and studios for artists, a number of which are dotted along Kalorama Road. A few of the older, small, specialized industrial shops also remain.

At 1770 Euclid Street, home of the First Church of Christ, Scientist, plans are now underway for the construction of a modern mid-sized hotel on the church's property. The plans, as approved, will incorporate the impressive and classic church building into the new project's overall design, thus saving this historic structure. This venture, situated near the very center of Adams Morgan, is expected to add some more enduring and stronger economic development to the area.

Reed-Cooke has developed its own unofficial but distinct neighborhood voice, and its residents continue to be engaged in some debate over the merits of a number of proposed projects in the neighborhood. A few recent endeavors, such as the renovation of the H.D. Cooke Elementary School, have already

The First Church of Christ, Scientist at 1770 Euclid Street. *Photo by the author.*

been successfully completed. Other newer proposals and projects, occurring as part of the city's ongoing life and activity, continue to generate this active discussion today, with opinions both pro and con. And some people in the neighborhood are currently considering presenting the area's residents with a plan to form and designate a new "Conservation District" for Reed-Cooke, or even possibly seeking to receive the more complex and challenging "historic district" designation. The neighborhood continues to evolve.

EAST OF THE PARK

Today, the area east of the park, especially to the southeast, has developed into a small community, which—situated at the juncture of several larger neighborhoods—has worked to create its own identity. An area that is largely residential, its citizens have formed the Meridian Hill Neighborhood Association. This relatively new community group is intended for the immediate area located around Meridian Hill Park, mainly just southeast of the park, from Sixteenth Street over to Twelfth Street, up to Chapin Street and down to U Street. The name makes a reasonable amount of sense for the locale, since the neighborhood, consisting primarily of homes built around 1900, sits between several other named localities. To its north lies Columbia Heights, to its west is Adams Morgan and to the east is Pleasant Plains. (The name Pleasant Plains has returned to use and encompasses the area going toward Georgia Avenue. It was the original name for the eastern portion of the old large Holmead tract.) To the south is the U Street area, part of the greater neighborhood of Shaw, which covers a large vicinity that includes several smaller neighborhoods. The association is evidently taking the park for its name, however, since anything east of Fourteenth Street is not really part of old Meridian Hill. Information from the group's website tells that it seeks to maintain and promote the civic health of its area, and to develop and foster a friendly neighborhood.

Along Fourteenth Street is the area's business district, with its interesting history and current growth. And along the south there is U Street, which of course has its own fascinating and famous story of cultural events and business activities, old and new.

This part of Columbia Heights in general continues with its renewed growth, and continues to generate additional fresh interest in its neighborhood. On Fifteenth Street, some nicely made new apartment houses have been recently completed.

9

Meridian Hill's Legacy

In most histories of Washington, D.C., and its neighborhoods, including Meridian Hill, the people being discussed—the people who were responsible for the physical landscape that was created—were usually the wealthy or the ruling individuals in the particular points of time being reviewed. The obvious and basic reason for this is the fact that very often the only records that have come through are about these people and their activities. By and large, these individuals were the creators and doers, and very often were the key dynamic actors in the civic situations that developed. Some started from the "humble beginnings" often written about, and rose to positions where they were able to produce objects that have endured, or to have developed plans of lasting influence. Others were born into money, with a resulting education, or used society's structure to gain wealth and then chose to use the money well, either for public works or architecturally, or both. And the city now has the physical legacy of all this fine architecture, as well as a variety of good housing stock now sitting throughout the neighborhood.

Of course, an area's history involves much more than just the principal players. We must remember that the many thousands of people who have lived in this area over the years—and passed through the landscape of Meridian Hill—were also participants in the flow of events that make up the human history here. Most of these people were constructive, some were neutral and a few were even damaging. Many added lasting but anonymous contributions to the world that we now enjoy today. In the overall assessment, then, there were the many who were positive and the few who were negative;

yet this is also certainly the same case with the more prominent and affluent players in the events described here—most good, and a few not.

One's perspective can color one's perception of what is most appropriate when caring for a neighborhood and its residents—especially when looking ahead. How we use our already-built world now is a statement about how we want our society to be living in the future. For all of our fellow citizens, we should save and conserve the beauty of the past within our city—for everyone to see, to be involved with, and to enjoy. But however we look at Meridian Hill, it does seem that the area, past and present, functions as a microcosm of the larger world that we all inhabit.

10

Meridian Hill's Future

A variety of factors will be at work creating the new pages of this area's continuing story. With the uncertainty that now exists within so many aspects of the larger world, the residents of Meridian Hill will need to continue supporting the basic work that is necessary to maintain their neighborhood, and, along with other Washingtonians, also need to continue supporting the city as a whole. The District government has been actively replacing some infrastructure components in the local neighborhood and is to be commended for this work. Water pipes, some dating back to the time of the initial development of the subdivision, have recently been replaced; other utilities should likewise be more closely evaluated and properly maintained.

For a city to thrive, its neighborhoods need to be vigorous and happy. For a nation to thrive, its citizens should use its resources thoughtfully and plan for a future that includes everyone. The United States, as a whole, has the technological knowhow to create a comfortable and secure life for all of its citizens, but unfortunately, this is not now being done, quite a bit hangs on important decisions to be made in the near future.

Historically, good cities have been balanced, organic places—not only being locations for work but also providing proper homes to the various groups of people who are part of the urban makeup of these cities. The old Meridian Hill subdivision was a nice example of this, with homes in a broad range, from the very wealthy to the average Joe plumbers. The citizens of the neighborhood today might do well to remember this simple, basic point and then consider how to best work at having a healthy and diverse urban culture exist—for all who now live and work here in the city.

In Meridian Hill today, just a fairly few spots of the old estate's land now remain vacant, or are being only slightly used. It might make good sense to continue adding homes for some new residents—perhaps including middle-income people who would bring various sorts of positive features to the city. Making this happen would probably take a measure of planning in order to create a range of homes and home prices because, looking ahead, it is likely that the area, with such an attractive location, will naturally draw wealthier new residents.

And of course, the balance between having entertainment and business in the city, and maintaining a reasonable and enjoyable place in which to live, is always one of the challenges of civic life: How much business? How much residential? This is something that Meridian Hill residents will no doubt have to continue to look at and discuss, and decide on—with the community subsequently moving forward into the planning and the implementation of any future changes. In addition, the larger question that comes with development—what of the present should be saved, and what should be jettisoned so that new, and perhaps more intensely urban construction might then be allowed to occur—is an issue for the community to definitely consider. And the same outside forces that helped to first build the neighborhood will continue to be major factors, as will the country's increasing population. What is saved depends not only on what the community wants to keep, but also, more importantly, on what the community is able to save. And the overall visual appearance of the area is another factor to be taken into account when looking at changes and growth.

There is also an important need to engage the newer members of the community, those who have recently moved to the new developments—mostly young people who very often have never before been personally involved with the dynamics of an urban community, and whose social contact is primarily done through the electronic world. Keeping local residents interested in working on their neighborhood is increasingly difficult in this age of isolated personal electronics. And at the other end of the human condition, the area has a growing number of NORC residents, those growing older in place and not wanting to head for an old-folk's home (NORC = naturally occurring retirement community). Getting different groups together can be a challenge. In the end, active, open and well-considered citizen participation within a democratic framework is nearly always the best approach for running any neighborhood.

And remember: to borrow a remark made by the character Doc Brown in the film *Back to the Future*, "Your future is whatever you make it, so make it a good one."

***

On the following pages are some notes, some photographs, and some pieces of related historical information, along with a few brief stories about the neighborhood around Meridian Hill. The history of any specific locale is almost always intertwined with that of its neighbors, and this is indeed the case with Meridian Hill.

11

Some Related Information

T he following items might well have been incorporated into the preceding narrative, but each of these brief pieces seems to be able to stand on its own as an interesting morsel of Washington history.

The Washington Meridian Stone

The Washington Meridian stone was a small finished stone marker that was set in 1804 as one of the indicators of the official meridian that had been surveyed by Thomas Jefferson; it was located in what is now the roadway of Sixteenth Street, due north of the White House, on Meridian Hill.

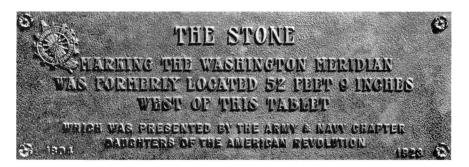

The plaque on the western wall of Meridian Hill Park, marking the site of the original meridian stone. *U.S. Commission of Fine Arts.*

The Washington City Race Course

This racetrack, known by several names (often simply as Holmead's), was one of the early city's main places of outdoor entertainment. Located on the wide plateau that extends north from today's Euclid Street (after the rise of Meridian Hill), it was circular, one mile in circumference, sitting on the northern side of Taylor's Lane Road, between present-day Eleventh and Sixteenth Streets. The track's main entrance was centered where Fourteenth Street Road came up and met Taylor's Lane Road. Laid out by Dr. William Thornton (an avid horseman) for John Tayloe and the once-famous Washington Jockey Club, the course was created in 1802 and lasted until about the mid-1840s, when beginning development in the area made its continued use impractical. The center of the circle appears to have been at just about the location of today's Fourteenth Street and Park Road. Spectators viewed the races from inside the track, entering mainly from the south. The different social classes had their own areas, and there was some seating, but evidently many fans would seek out their own viewing spots in a sort of festival atmosphere. Contemporary writers report that at times Congress, after having sat through a particularly arduous session, would adjourn, and then many of its members would travel up the hill to relax and attend the horse races there.

The Size of the Meridian Hill Estate

The property's original area has at times been reported to have been larger than its 110¼ acres, with 157 acres on occasion being cited as the size. This number may have come from the total acreage of the two—but separate—properties that shared the land on the hill north above Boundary Street: the Porter estate's spread of 110¼ acres, plus the adjoining tract of 46½ acres that composed Columbian College. Together, they add up to the 157 acres. This demonstrates a situation that can sometimes occur over time and in almost any locale; that is, two or more distinct but neighboring entities may become historically blended together as the past gets condensed.

Peter L'Enfant and His Name in History

In fairness to Peter L'Enfant, our collective historical record should be referring to him as he wanted to be known. "Pierre" has been the name more often used in writings about L'Enfant, but this noted architect and city planner proudly took the name "Peter" after coming to America. Arriving in 1777 to fight in the American War of Independence, L'Enfant became a captain in the Corps of Engineers, later attaining the rank of major. Talented, well educated and famously temperamental, Peter L'Enfant assisted George Washington in the war, and then worked successfully as an architect and designer before being selected by the president to be the main planner of the new federal city. The vision and enthusiasm of this man were crucial factors in the initial design of Washington, D.C. Even before he began work on his famous plan for the city, L'Enfant had proudly taken the name Peter, using it rather than Pierre, to proclaim that he was moving forward into the great adventure upon which the United States was embarking. Thereafter and throughout his life, in personal and official correspondence he was known as Peter. It was only in the late nineteenth century, when his reputation was being publicly resurrected, that the common misperception was created (and was then promoted by the French ambassador to the United States) that Pierre should be the correct first name for Mr. L'Enfant. So as historian Kenneth Bowling has noted, using Peter when writing about L'Enfant more accurately and properly describes this noted gentleman. (Reference: Kenneth R. Bowling, *Peter Charles L'Enfant: Vision, Honor and Male Friendship in the Early American Republic*, 2002)

The Neighbors in 1830

A snapshot of the area directly around Meridian Hill in the year 1830, when the property was purchased by Justice J.F. Cox, would have shown the following:

To the south, below Boundary Street, was the upper part of the federal city with its planned grid of streets, but still mostly undeveloped and sparsely inhabited—it was almost empty for many blocks going south. Not much had been built north of K Street, but some pieces of land were being lightly farmed. Also, a bit west along Boundary Street, at its southwest corner with Nineteenth Street, and just inside the city limits, was the old Holmead's Cemetery, a local resting place that had been taken over by the city and renamed Western Burial Ground. (It was closed in 1870, and by 1880 those buried there had been relocated.)

On the east was Columbia College, founded in 1821, with its land going over to Fourteenth Street Road; in December 1824, it had graduated its first class (of three!). The college was struggling financially and had on its property in 1830 one large building along with just a few other smaller ones.

And then directly east on the other side of Fourteenth Street Road, was the William J. Stone estate and farm—this 121-acre tract, purchased by Stone in 1815, had been part of the broad Mount Pleasant expanse owned by the Peter family. Stone was a renowned engraver who worked on reproducing and then printing copies of the Declaration of Independence.

To the north, across Taylor's Lane Road and around where Sixteenth Street runs today, sat the Eslin farm and the tavern, which had been built in 1826. James Eslin had earlier purchased this forty-acre tract for a farm, later adding a "Public House," which was widely known for gambling. The Eslin family became related to the Holmeads by marriage and remained close friends with them, bringing life and fun to the Holmead environment. Immediately east of the tavern was the popular city racetrack, a one-mile circular course laid out in 1802 by Dr. William Thornton on land leased by the Jockey Club from the Holmeads. The entrance to the track was located where Fourteenth Street Road came up and met Taylor's Lane Road. Farther to the north was additional Holmead property.

On the west, across the property-line creek, was the Hines farm, where brothers Christian and Matthew were engaged in their business plan to raise silkworms. With the area's climate not entirely suitable for this activity, the scheme eventually failed when the silkworms did not thrive and the two lost the farm six years later. The brothers had purchased the land in 1828 from Dr. William Thornton's widow, Anna Maria, who had sold it immediately after William's death, likely to settle some of her husband's debts. The doctor had obtained this land from Robert Peter and had used it as a horse farm. Dr. Thornton was a Washington physician and noted architect of many of the city's early buildings and most famously the first architect of the U.S. Capitol.

So began Meridian Hill's neighborhood.

JAMES HOLMEAD

The early colonial history of Meridian Hill's territory has many aspects to it and was certainly a dynamic time. One fundamental issue from that era, of course, is the question of by what right did the English lay claim to the lands that they took and then planted with new settlers. After all, the Native Americans were there, and the early so-called land-purchase-deals—often conducted under deceptive circumstances with these native people—were many times not even clearly defined transactions. So this is a valid question, but since the basic real-estate ownership system of the United States is founded on these royal land grants and claims, the issue is essentially moot. We live today with what we have received. Times, it seems, were different then. Simply declaring that the native inhabitants were not the possessors was enough. Using a system of "planting" people on newly annexed territory had been loosely practiced by the British Crown when subjugating Ireland and other areas, from the 1200s up until just before 1600, when the practice became more effectively organized and systematically carried out. So it was a logical extension for the English, and other countries, to use the same procedure when colonizing America. But the past has occurred, of course; we can best use it as an aid to understand our current world and then work to progressively plan the future.

Within the lands of this large royal charter that became the Maryland colony, the first settlers—the planters—not only had to completely set up their own lives but also had to deal with the Native Americans, as well as with the other settlers from across the Potomac in Virginia, who were at times claiming the Maryland lands and even trying to take the Maryland tracts by force. Further, the Marylanders had to contend with the political turmoil that was occurring back in England in the mid-1600s, and with the subsequent swings in the control of the colony that took place. And then, they had to deal with one another.

So in the early 1700s, when James Holmead arrived in the Maryland territory, most of the land was still undeveloped. At first, ownership of some of the large tracts of the land there was not always a settled issue, but there are many records that still exist; some of these documents are quite clear and some conflicting or obscurely defined. Many tracts are merely described by name, such as Valentine's Garden. James is listed in a number of these land records of Prince George's County, dating from 1711, with several variations in the spelling of his last name. In these records, he is registered at different times as a planter or as a gentleman, or with no descriptive appellation, and was capable of signing his name. He was likely able to read and write, since he was sometimes listed as a witness on other transaction documents where one or more of the parties involved could only make his or her mark.

James entered into agreements with other planters and farmers, one instance being with his neighbor John Flint, with whom he co-owned some land. John was recorded as being a yeoman (a farmer who owns and works his own tract of land and an individual socially a bit below a gentleman). Both John and James were vestrymen at Rock Creek Church, the community's social and civic center; the parish, established in 1712, is still located on its original church land, which now also holds the noted Rock Creek Cemetery. Other Holmead transactions involved the Beall family, later of Georgetown prominence; the Bealls had a stretch of land along Rock Creek, abutting a portion of his property. James Holmead appears to have been a solid and trusted member of this early society, and it might be said that he played well with others.

In the area of the District's present-day Ward One, Holmead had most of his landholdings; he additionally was recorded as possessing (at various times) other pieces of property about fifteen miles north of Georgetown and inland from the Potomac. And although some of these areas (as described in the original land records) are among the imprecisely defined transactions, James definitely held a good number of tracts of land.

His initial purchase in the Rock Creek area appears to have been a 206-acre portion of the old Widow's Mite tract, which had been sold to him by Thomas Fletchall in 1722. Not long thereafter, in a key purchase in 1733, James entered into an agreement with settler Thomas Lamarr to acquire two tracts (Bealls Plaine and Lamarr's Outlet) totaling 935 acres, just east and south of the confluence of Rock Creek and Piney Branch Creek. (Thomas Lamarr's father, also Thomas, had come to the area in 1663 and claimed several pieces of land; he passed away in 1714. Thomas Jr., after selling these two local tracts to Holmead, later moved north along the Potomac.) James added additional smaller tracts, too. In the early frontier, land was a commodity that was traded almost in the same manner in which other goods were bought and sold. As an example of the local value of land at that time, that 206-acre tract purchased by Holmead in 1722 was sold for the price of thirty-eight pounds.

James Holmead, with spelling variants such as Holmeard, appears to be the first effective settler of the land in this local area. Below is a key event, his 1722 land acquisition (often mistakenly listed as occurring in 1727), which apparently established the core of his property in the region:

> Prince George's Land Records 1717–1726
> Indenture, 4 Mar 1722; enrolled 3 Apr 1723
>> From: Thomas Fletchall, planter of Prince George's County
>> To: James Holmeard, planter of Prince George's County
>> For £38 a tract of land being part of a tract called Widow's Mite
>> on the Potomac in prince George's County; containing 206 acres
>> /s/ Thomas Fletchall

Part of the land that James possessed went all the way over to Rock Creek, and then north along the creek for a short stretch, this being on the north side of the old main road (Rock Creek Road) and located where the road exited Georgetown and crossed the creek, going northeast. This crossing occurred just south of today's P Street Bridge, at the spot that is now known as the P Street Beach (and which is a visibly good location for a crossing). On his land along the creek bank there, in about 1740 James reportedly built a small flour mill that was likely one of the earliest mills in the general area.

James was recorded as marrying twice, first to Mary Hallum, and then to Elizabeth Meares, who survived him. And he had a son, James Jr., who apparently lived on Holmead land in what is now central Montgomery County, Maryland. In about 1754, James the father passed away (in late 1754, Elizabeth was carrying out the provisions of his will); his son may have also passed on about this time, since he fades from the civil records. In any case, the elder James also had a nephew, Anthony Holmead, who had come over from England in 1750 and to whom James willed his estate. After inheriting this large, local Rock Creek–area set of tracts—which as of 1735 had totaled nearly two square miles—Anthony effectively tended to his new property so that when he died in 1802, his holdings were quite large. One piece, located directly north of the federal city, was of 595 acres and was known as Pleasant Plains, named by the Holmeads. These holdings generally extended east toward today's Georgia Avenue, where they abutted the property of others,

Holmead Manor, dating from 1740, was located near today's Thirteenth Street and Otis Place. It sat on the northern part of their land and was the earliest permanent home for the family. (Photo circa 1885.) *Historical Society of Washington, D.C.*

such as the Petworth estate. On the west side, Anthony's land continued to spread over right to Rock Creek near Georgetown; he additionally owned scattered blocks within the newly organized city—traded in exchange for the part of his land that was taken for the city.

Thus, looking at the land of today's Ward One—and with the exception of several tracts, such as the large one south of today's Columbia Road, which was land once owned by John Flint—a good percentage of the ward was originally Holmead property. Beginning with James, the Holmeads were among the first modern occupants of this key section of the city. They used the land by farming it, building several homes and establishing a cemetery. They added to the neighborhood, and then passed the land along to others.

And so, because of James Holmead's contributions to the area's spirit and history, it would seem appropriate that there should be some sort of local memorial to him. Perhaps this is something to consider for the future.

COLUMBIA ROAD

Now the main route across Adams Morgan, this major thoroughfare was part of old Rock Creek Road. This is a road with a history, one that includes having several different names. From the time of its earliest existence to the present day, this old and well-used pathway has had a number of name changes. Here is a listing of these various designations, with approximate dates of use. Of course, in the general day-to-day functioning of civic life, the names used for the road would surely have often overlapped. So, beginning with the earliest:

An Old Native American Trail

The original path ran along a ridge, ascending and following along the edge of a wide plateau; the land of this plateau now holds a large part of the central area of Washington. The route was useful because it traveled along a watershed divide, with no streams crossing its path. (Dates: from a long time back, perhaps seven thousand years ago, to about the colonial-era year of 1700.)

Rock Creek Road

This was one of the very earliest roads in the region. After the river landing that became Georgetown was established and the nearby tracts of land were first being settled—shortly after 1700—the route developed out of necessity. In 1719, Rock Creek Church was built at the site of today's historic Rock Creek Cemetery. (The parish had been established in 1712.) The road ran from Georgetown up and over to the church, and then continued toward the north, skirting the valley of Piney Branch Creek. In what is now Northeast D.C., the road generally followed the logical path north, using close to the same route taken by the main railroad line that currently runs into the city. This path along that stretch, now Blair Road, proceeded north and exited the District at what would much later become Silver Spring. The route then branched and went either north to the small local villages such as Brookeville, or toward the northeast and on to Baltimore. (Dates: 1700–1780.)

(And in the area of today's Adams Morgan, separately but from the same time, another early road ran along the base of the hill on which Rock Creek Road was situated. This route was the Georgetown–Bladensburg Road that ran east to Bladensburg and then on to Annapolis; part of it later became Florida Avenue.)

Rock Creek Church Road

As the area grew, other thoroughfares with more efficient long-distance travel paths came into use, and the road became more of a local route. Thus the church became the primary identifier of the road's purpose. (Dates: 1780–1810.)

Old Taylor's Lane

Part of the upper portion of the route going to the church became less used. One of the main reasons for then taking the road was to visit the large (one-mile-around) racetrack that John Tayloe had built in 1802 (at what is now Fourteenth Street and Columbia Road). In addition, farther up the road, near the church, Tayloe had established a large estate, which he named Petworth. Mapmakers "corrected" the spelling of "Tayloe" to "Taylor." (Dates: 1810–1840.)

Taylor's Lane Road

With local growth, and more use, traffic increased, and it became apparent that this was no longer really just a lane, so it acquired the more descriptive word road. Its through-route north also became interrupted east of today's Fourteenth Street, where the old road had turned north near the present-day Eleventh Street, and so when going out to Rock Creek Church, a turn onto Fourteenth Street Road was usually necessary. (Dates: 1840–1865.)

Georgetown Road

It had originally been the road from Georgetown, and the name Taylor's Lane Road was cumbersome and not all that stylish, so a new name was tried. (Dates: 1865–1880.)

Columbia Avenue

More thought: it didn't now go directly to Georgetown, which was not even close by, anyway. And more accurately, the road historically was used to go to Columbia College (officially "Columbian"), which was situated between Fourteenth and Fifteenth Streets on the south side of the road. Columbia was a good and honorable name. (Date: 1880.)

Columbia Road

After review, it appears that the city and its citizens realized that this route was no avenue: it wasn't fancy or straight. It was a necessity. It was a road. And so it received the name by which it has been known as for the past 130 years: Columbia Road. And as the city grew, its direction was realigned east of Fourteenth Street, and the road was then developed as part of an important east–west city traffic route. (Dates: 1880–present.)

Columbia Road is a great road, full of life, running from Connecticut Avenue on the west, through the center of Adams Morgan, and into Columbia Heights, then (with Harvard Street) over across to Georgia Avenue and past the McMillan Reservoir, becoming Michigan Avenue and continuing on as part of a major mid-city crosstown artery.

The castle, abandoned, shortly before its end. *Library of Congress, Theodor Horydczak Collection.*

MARY HENDERSON AND A FINAL STORY

In February 1931, Mary was eighty-nine and had lived a long and famously productive life. At this time, she had just recently again offered to give what was perhaps her finest mansion to the United States government for use as the official residence of the vice president. This gift of the property at 2801 Sixteenth Street was later again politely declined—it was thought to be too grand for that elected position and too expensive to maintain. This striking mansion would eventually become the embassy of Spain. But now, Mary was in the news and appearing in court to testify at a formal proceeding concerning this offer of hers, and the legal challenge that had been brought by her adoptive granddaughter. Her granddaughter was asserting that Mary had become mentally unfit and thus should not be allowed to even offer such gift. Her granddaughter, then being Mary's sole remaining close relative (Mary's son had died in 1923 and his wife in 1907), no doubt had her eye on Mary's large estate.

Mary prevailed in court and most certainly was thoroughly displeased; she subsequently disowned her perhaps unwise granddaughter and then famously cut her out of the will.

The story of Mary and her granddaughter is in itself unusual and like something out of a Hollywood melodrama. John and Mary Henderson's only child—a son named John Jr.—had married, and the new couple then encountered problems conceiving a child. After the marriage, the elder Hendersons had promised John Jr. and his wife, Angelica, a substantial immediate gift when they produced an heir. So the young couple concocted an elaborate ruse: faking a pregnancy (with the works: padding, doctor visits, etc.) and then secretly adopting a newborn baby. All concerned were happy, until years later when Mary learned of the sham. She was, to say the least, distressed and not at all pleased. In time, however, Mary reconciled with her granddaughter, Beatrice, and quietly adopted her. Things apparently went well enough until the events of 1931. After Mary's death, her substantial estate (in the neighborhood of $6 million) was tied up in court for years; this unsettled situation may have been the primary reason why her prized castle was allowed to decline and, in the end, was never again to be enjoyed by anyone as the extraordinary home that it had once been.

The following is an excerpt from an article in *Time* magazine, February 25, 1935, titled "Art: Henderson Sale":

> To Washington society it was an occasion, to His Excellency Mehmet Munir Bey, Ambassador of the Turkish Republic, it was an opportunity. Last week, the pictures and knick knacks of Mrs. John Brooks Henderson's bulbous brownstone castle on 16th Street went on the auction block.
>
> Washington society has been the duller since Mrs. Henderson died in 1931, aged 90. Wealthy widow of the late Senator from Missouri and friend of Presidents Lincoln through Hoover inclusive, it was among her various ambitions to make 16th Street the social stem of Washington, D.C. Buying great quantities of real estate, she induced the Austrian, Spanish, Cuban, Polish, French and Lithuanian embassies to move there, built a $300,000 palace which she attempted time after time to have made the official home of the Vice Presidents of the U.S. Vegetarian, ardent prohibitionist (she poured her husband's valuable cellar into the gutter immediately after his death) and anti-tobacconist, she caused one great sensation in 1931 when she publicly announced that her granddaughter, Mrs. Beatrice ("Trixie") Van Rensselaer Henderson Wholean was a foundling, secretly adopted to inherit a $600,000 trust fund.

A view of the neighborhood today, on Euclid Street near Ontario Road. *Photo by the author.*

Selected Bibliography and Additional Sources

Among the books, articles and data repositories that were used as sources of information in creating this monograph are the following, explored with much appreciation:

Bowling, Kenneth R. *The Creation of Washington, D.C.* Washington, D.C.: George Mason University Press, 1991.

Brugger, Robert J. *Maryland, A Middle Temperment 1634–1980*. Baltimore: Johns Hopkins University Press, 1988.

Bryan, Wilhelmus Bogart. *A History of the National Capital from Its Foundation Through the Period of the Adoption of the Organic Act: 1815–1878*. New York: MacMillan Company, 1916.

Eliot, Jonathan. *Historical Sketches of the Ten Mile Square Forming the District of Columbia*. N.p.: J. Elliot Jr., 1830.

Emery, Fred. *Mount Pleasant and Meridian Hill*. Washington, D.C.: Records of the Columbia Historical Society, 1932.

Encyclopedia of Massachusetts, Biographical–Genealogical. N.p.: American Historical Society, 1916.

Gahn, Bessie Wilmarth. *Original Patentees of Land at Washington*. Baltimore: Clearfield Company, 1936.

Goode, James. *Best Addresses*. Washington, D.C.: Smithsonian Books, 2003.

Hines, Christian. *Early Recollections of Washington City*. Washington, D.C.: Junior League of Washington, 1866. Reprint, 1981.

Kayser, Elmer L. *Bricks Without Straw: The Evolution of George Washington University*. New York: Appleton-Century-Crofts, 1970.

King, Nicholas. *Peter Manuscript Atlas of Mount Pleasant and Mexico, D.C., 1788–1809*. N.p.: self-published, 1809.

Leeson, Michael A. *History of Kent County, Michigan*. Chicago: Charles C. Chapman, 1881.

Marberry, M. Marion. *Splendid Poseur: Joaquin Miller, American Poet*. Boston: Thomas Y. Crowell Company, 1953.

Porter, David Dixon. *Memoir of Commodore David Porter, of the United States Navy*. Albany, NY: J. Munsell, 1875

Scharf, J. Thomas. *History of Western Maryland*. Philadelphia: Louis H. Everts, 1882.

Williams, C.S. *Descendants of John Cox*. N.p.: self-published, 1909.

Williams, Kim Prothro. "Meridian Hill Historic District." National Register of Historic Places registration form. Washington, D.C.: Government Printing Office, 2014.

Additional Sources

District of Columbia Government
    D.C. Public Library, Washingtoniana Collection
    Office of Planning, and Historic Preservation Office
    Office of the Surveyor (Department of Consumer and Regulatory Affairs)
    Recorder of Deeds
George Washington University and its publications
Historical Society of Washington, D.C.
Library of Congress
National Archives
National Park Service and its publications
Prince George's County: Land Records Division
Reference publications of Wesley E. Pippenger
Time magazine
U.S. Commission of Fine Arts
Washington Evening Star newspaper

Index

About the Author

S teve McKevitt was born in Washington, D.C. (a native Washingtonian!), and grew up locally in Silver Spring, Maryland. After living in Wisconsin for a time, he returned to the District and for many years worked for the federal government. Recently retired, he is now involved in exploring the various aspects of Washington's civic and cultural history. He is also a member of the Historical Society of Washington, D.C., as well as several local community associations. His continuing interest in our collective past has been motivated by a number of factors; he warmly recalls the eager curiosity that he felt as a very young child when he was first told and then comprehended that everything already done has a history, and that very often there are some great stories, fun and illuminating, sitting within this past time. That, and having some good teachers.

Visit us at
www.historypress.net
....

This title is also available as an e-book